THEOSOPHY

THEOSOPHY

RUDOLF STEINER

An Introduction to the Spiritual Processes

in Human Life and in the Cosmos

Translated by CATHERINE E. CREEGER

🖋 ANTHROPOSOPHIC PRESS

The first English edition of this work was published by Kegan Paul, London, and Rand McNally, Chicago, in 1910. A new edition was published by Kegan Paul in 1922 and a further new translation from the final German revised edition (19th) by the Rudolf Steiner Publishing Co., London, and Anthroposophic Press, New York, [Anthroposophical Literary Concern] in 1922. In 1932 a new translation was published by the Rudolf Steiner Publishing Co., London, and Anthroposophic Press, New York, which was revised in 1954 and further revised in 1965. In 1946 the Anthroposophic Press published a translation by Henry B. Monges, which was revised by Gilbert Church in 1971.

This volume is a translation of *Theosophie, Einführung in übersinnliche Welterkenntnis und Menschenbestimmung* (vol. 9 in the Bibliographic Survey, 1961) published by Rudolf Steiner Verlag, Dornach, Switzerland.

This edition Copyright © 1994 by Anthroposophic Press.
Introduction Copyright © 1994 by Michael Holdrege.

Published by Anthroposophic Press
www.steinerbooks.org

Library of Congress Cataloging-in-Publication Data

Steiner, Rudolf, 1861–1925.
    [Theosophie. English]
    Theosophy ; an introduction to the spiritual processes at work
in human life and in the cosmos / Rudolf Steiner.
        p. cm.—(Classics in anthroposophy)
    Includes bibliographical references and index.
    ISBN 0-88010-373-6
    1. Anthroposophy.   I. Title.   II. Series.
BP595.S894T4713   1994   93-35871
299'.934—dc20   CIP

Cover design: Barbara Richey

Ninth printing, 2008

Printed in the United States of America by McNaughton & Gunn, Inc.

CONTENTS

Chapter 3

THE THREE WORLDS   *93*

Chapter 4

THE PATH TO KNOWLEDGE   *175*

I

A third of a century has now passed since C. P. Snow brought to wider awareness a crisis simmering just below the surface of Western cultural life. In his Rede lectures at Cambridge University Snow spoke of "two cultures" existing side by side within one culture, yet separated by a yawning gulf. Not only was communication very limited between the groups Snow chose to characterize—the scientists and the literary intellectuals—but a somewhat hostile mood even existed. Have we lost even the pretense of a common culture? This was the question Snow placed before the Western world.

When Snow raised this question, the belief in continued progress through the consequent application of science and technology to society's problems and needs was still borne with tremendous optimism. Viewed from the perspective of the 1990s, the polarization he was pointing to seems barely to have surfaced at the time he spoke. Today this gulf is evident everywhere—but in much greater diversity and at many different levels: from multiculturalism to postmodernity. Many additional "cultures" have since raised their voices in the great debate about the future of humanity.

A major impetus in this direction was given in the early sixties by Thomas Kuhn's book *The Structure of Scientific Revolutions*. In what is probably the most widely discussed analysis of the scientific endeavor in the second half of this century, Kuhn makes evident the presuppositions that underlie every form of scientific activity. Scientific "truths," supposedly "objective" in nature, were shown to be the reflection of a background of shared assumptions dominant in that scientific community. Kuhn called this framework of presuppositions a "paradigm." When a paradigm changes, so does the appearance of the world for those sharing that viewpoint.

What Kuhn formulated in the context of modern science has, together with its wider implications for nonscientific discourse, shaken the rationalistic foundations of Western society at the end of this century. The suspicion has emerged that all thought and belief systems are merely social constructions. Sometimes known as our "postmodern condition," this situation is characterized by a plurality of viewpoints—not just Snow's two cultures—where varying groups are often unable to communicate with each other because of the different "languages" they speak. Not only has the legitimacy of scientific knowledge as the primary source of "objective" understanding been called into question, but also the possibility of making valid universal statements about the nature of anything.

Whereas the latter discussion has taken place primarily at an academic level, the crisis of "modernism" has become evident throughout Western society. Be it in economics, in education, in environmental or in social issues, we find ourselves at the dawn of a new millennium in the midst of a multifaceted reconsideration of our cultural foundations. Like it or not, the limits of reductive natural science and of the narrow fixation on outer progress are becoming undeniably visible. For many individuals this has led to a shift in perspective. An awareness is growing today that the problems we face did not "fall from Heaven," but result from human deeds, the source of which lies in human consciousness. To look at the "outer" state of the world we have created is to see a reflection of our own "inner" state. This perspective is clearly reflected in Albert Gore's widely read book *Earth in the Balance*. Gore speaks of the profound separation that has arisen in the course of Western cultural history between our intellect and the physical world in which we live. He sees this as a major source of the unhealthy relationship to our natural environment which is visible in the ecological crisis we face today.

In light of such fundamental reflections on the foundations of Western culture arising in our time, future generations may well express surprise at the relative unfamiliarity of today's American public with the work of Rudolf Steiner; for Steiner devoted his whole life to overcoming the gulf arising between science, art, and religion, between clear scientific thinking and the belief in "higher" realities. He did this in a manner that recognizes the inadequacy of monolithic world views, in which everything is subsumed under a universal principle. Already at the age of twenty-five Steiner had formulated the nature of this problem, and had shown in reference to the German poet and scientist Goethe, a much wider perspective:

> Goethe's world view is the most many-sided imaginable. It issues from a center resting within the unified nature of the poet, and it always turns outward the side corresponding to the nature of the object being considered. The unity of the spiritual forces being exercised lies in Goethe's nature; the *way* these forces are exercised at any given moment is determined by the object under consideration. Goethe takes his way of looking at things from the outer world and does not force any particular way upon it. These days, however, the thinking of many people is active in only *one* particular way; it is useful for only one category of objects; it is not, like that of Goethe, *unified* but rather *uniform*.... Goethe's world view encompasses many directions of thought in the sense just indicated and cannot, in fact, ever be imbued with any single, one-sided conception.
>
> (*The Science of Knowing*, pp.14-15)

What Steiner characterizes in regard to Goethe's world view is true to an even larger extent of his own.

But Rudolf Steiner was not only a thinker. His multi-dimensional approach to questions of practical life has also borne significant fruit. Steiner was, in fact, the founder of numerous impulses for the renewal of human society: from the largest nonsectarian school movement in the world today—Waldorf education—to the creation of new forms of organic agriculture, holistic medicine, pharmacology and education for the developmentally handicapped. Not only was he a pioneer in the realm of the arts and architecture, but his ideas have also stimulated new approaches in banking and organizational development. How, future generations may ask, could a man capable of initiating such numerous impulses relevant to the crisis of modern civilization remain almost unknown in twentieth-century America?

That more people are searching for new ways of thinking and for new approaches to the multiplying challenges of modern life is clearly apparent after a ten-minute visit to the corner bookstore. But among the hundreds of books one finds little or no Steiner. One explanation for this relative scarcity can be found by comparing his writings with those otherwise available to the searching reader.

Rudolf Steiner's books and published lecture cycles reveal themselves, upon closer scrutiny, to be difficult reading. In our culture of the "quick-fix," the effort required to work through a book by Steiner will seem excessive to many. Yet it is just this difficulty which gives his writings much of their value. The central task of this introduction to Steiner's *Theosophy* will be to shed light upon this aspect of his writings. Hence we shall return repeatedly to the question of why he wrote in the way he did, in order to see more clearly what his intentions were.

II

There are many entryways into the work of Rudolf Steiner. In fact, the confrontation with a collected works of over 360 volumes (a great number of which are available in English) can be quite dismaying for the potential student. *Theosophy* is one good starting point; Steiner himself called it an introduction. Nonetheless he is careful to point out that the words of Goethe with which chapter 1 begins are "the *starting point* of *one* of the paths that lead to being able to recognize the true nature of the human being" (italics added). *Theosophy* is a starting point, and it is the exposition of one possible way to approach the human riddle. Such an observation is characteristic of Rudolf Steiner. Throughout his books and lecture cycles he continually approaches fundamental questions of human existence from new and different perspectives. He was a consistent opponent of dogmatically held views that seek to frame the depths of reality in rigid systems of thought. This is important to keep in mind when reading *Theosophy*, for it is but one of the ways in which Steiner approaches the questions dealt with there. Rudolf Steiner published *Theosophy* after two decades as a researcher and author,[1] primarily in the fields of philosophy and the theory of science. It was a surprise to many.

---

1. During these two decades he was the editor of Goethe's natural scientific works in two major editions, the editor of a twelve-volume edition of Schopenhauer's works and of an eight-volume edition of Jean Paul.

Known as a prodigious student of past and modern thought, he seemed to have suddenly overstepped the boundaries of accepted scientific thinking.

This reaction did not surprise Steiner. He was, after all, an expert on questions of scientific method. In fact, it was just this issue that he consciously raised with this book: Have the limits of scientific discourse been rightfully drawn?

He characterized his spiritual scientific method (which he later called Anthroposophy) as one that "in the full sense of the word recognizes and supports the current view of natural scientific research where it is justified. On the other hand it strives through the rigorous and ordered training of purely inward (soul) faculties to achieve exact and objective results about supersensible realms of existence. It gives validity only to those results won by inner soul observation, in which the soul-spiritual organization can be grasped and overviewed as exactly as a mathematical problem." (*Cosmology, Religion and Philosophy*, pp.7-8, translation Michael Holdrege).

---

1. (*continued*) He was editor in chief of the *Journal for Literature* in Berlin for several years, and his cultural and scientific essays written for various journals within this period fill five volumes totalling approximately three thousand pages. In addition to these activities he authored eight books during this phase of his life: *The Science of Knowing, Truth and Knowledge, The Philosophy of Freedom, Friedrich Nietzsche—Fighter for Freedom, Goethe's World Conception, Mysticism at the Dawn of the Modern Age, The Occult Movement in the Nineteenth Century,* and *Christianity as Mystical Fact.*

Rudolf Steiner was acutely aware not only of the significance of modern scientific thought, but also of its limitations. He strove to overcome the reduction of the scientifically knowable world to those aspects of reality accessible only to outer empiricism and mathematical quantification, while at the same time upholding the rigor and objectivity that distinguishes science from opinion.

But to expand the scientific method into deeper aspects of existence is not a simple matter. It demands the careful and exacting training of faculties that are for the most part dormant in the human soul today. Rudolf Steiner went to considerable pains to characterize the way in which such faculties can be developed;[2] for without such training the possibilities for error and illusion are immense. It is before this background that *Theosophy* appears as one way by which the essential nature of human beings can be known.

The demands of spiritual science are present not only for the researcher; demands are also made of the reader. As *Theosophy* unfolds, dimensions of human existence not accessible to "everyday" experience are revealed, presenting a significant challenge to the reader. If he or

---

2. In the lecture cycle *The Boundaries of Natural Science*, for example, he frames this task in the context of modern science. A more general exposition of these issues is in *How to Know Higher Worlds* (previously, *Knowledge of the Higher Worlds and Its Attainment*), which gives a short introduction to these questions in the last chapter.

she is to find a fruitful relationship to such supersensible observations, a new kind of reading is necessary. As Steiner says in the Preface to the Third Edition:

> This book cannot be read the way people ordinarily read books in this day and age. In some respects, its readers will have to work their way through each page and even each single sentence the hard way. This was done deliberately; it is the only way this book can become what it is intended to be for the reader. Simply reading it through is as good as not reading it at all. The spiritual scientific truths it contains must be experienced; that is the only way they can be of value.

The book is consciously written in a manner that requires enhanced activity by the reader. "...its readers will have to work their way through each page and even each single sentence...", which is to say, that the contents are not painless injections of spiritual knowledge, to be received effortlessly and directly into the flow of the reader's consciousness. But rather it is what the reader "does" that is of primary significance. To become inwardly active to an extent far beyond that required by most reading is the challenge of Rudolf Steiner's books. If we read *Theosophy* in an everyday manner, it can appear to be nothing but a systematic description of sensible and supersensible members of the human being, a description that can be believed or not believed, depending on one's disposition.

Steiner was clear about this:

> I have often pointed out that there are two ways of reading a book like my *Theosophy*. One is to read, "The human being consists of physical body, etheric body, astral body, etc. and lives repeated earth lives and has a karma, etc." A reader of this kind is taking in concepts. They are, of course, rather different concepts than one finds elsewhere, but the mental process that is going on is in many respects identical with what takes place when one studies a cookbook. My point was exactly that the *process* is the important thing, not the absorption of ideas. It makes no difference whether you are reading, "Put butter into a frying pan, add flour, stir; add the beaten eggs, etc." or, "There is physical matter, etheric forces, astral forces, and they interpenetrate each other." It is all one from the standpoint of the soul process involved whether butter, eggs, and flour are being mixed at a stove or the human entelechy is conceived as a mixture of physical, etheric, and astral bodies.
>
> But one can also read *Theosophy* in such a manner as to realize that it contains concepts that stand in the same relation to the world of ordinary physical concepts as the latter does to the dream world. They belong to a world to which one has to *awaken* out of the ordinary physical realm in just the way one wakes out of one's dream world into the physical. It is the *attitude* one has in reading that gives things the right coloring.
>
> (*Awakening to Community*, p. 158, italics added)

Steiner does not simply give a systematic "cookbook" description of the human being at different levels of existence. The concepts presented at the beginning of the book grow, differentiate, and develop in a manner that easily goes unnoticed to the casual reader. What appear at first to be mere definitions reveal themselves to careful study as many-faceted realities of human existence, which undergo a "metamorphosis" as the book progresses. To enter into the expansion and transformation of these ideas, to make the subtle observations necessary to ground them in one's own experience, is not easy. It requires a heightened level of activity and concentration.

And yet it is just in this "more," which a book such as *Theosophy* necessitates, that its deeper fruitfulness for us lies. We begin to exercise those faculties of cognition which allow us with time to experience the realms of existence spoken of by Rudolf Steiner. Just as a muscle grows only through abnormal demands put upon it, so, in a similar manner, do our inner faculties as well.

III

Chapter 1 of *Theosophy* begins with the trichotomy of body, soul and spirit. Although appearing to revive antique distinctions about the human organization, Steiner is careful to point out that whoever associates preconceived notions with these three words will necessarily misunderstand what is meant. These concepts are to be understood only through subtle observation of the phenomena themselves.

Further reading shows that the human being is not simply made up of body, soul and spirit (and their further differentiations), but exists as a unique individuality—an "I" —that is active within these three regions of its being. This individuality is not simply the sum of its parts, it is an active transformative agent within them.

What we know as our "I" at our current level of development is but a beginning. What Steiner points to in the concepts "spirit self," "life spirit," and "spirit body" is the largely untapped potentiality of the human "I" to penetrate ever more deeply its soul and bodily nature, spiritualizing and individualizing them in the process. The picture that arises in chapter 1 is of the human being in an evolutive process of becoming, with the agent of transformation being the activity of the "I" itself. Discovering this possibility in oneself is the first step in the conscious realization of this potentiality. In the words of Johannes Tauler, "If I were King in a land and did not know it, I would not be King." Chapter 1 seeks, among other things, to bring this largely dormant "Kingship" to our awareness.

IV

Building on his description of the differentiated nature of the human being, Steiner attempts to show in chapter 2 the extent to which it is possible to speak of repeated earth lives and destiny on the basis of experiences accessible to ordinary human consciousness. This is a very difficult undertaking, as Steiner was well aware. Many years later he commented on the challenges this section of the book presented him:

> For one who wishes to remain scientific the presentation of repeated earth lives becomes very difficult.... If it is not desired at this point to speak merely out of spiritual perceptions, it is necessary to resort to ideas which result, to be sure, from a subtle observation of the sense-world, but which people fail to grasp. For such a more subtle way of observing, the human being is seen to be different in organization and evolution from the animal world. And, if this fact of difference is observed, life itself gives rise to the idea of repeated earthly lives. But no attention is paid to this: hence such ideas seem not to have been taken from life, but to have been conceived arbitrarily or simply picked up out of more ancient views.
>
> I faced these difficulties in full consciousness. I battled with them. Any one who will take the trouble to review the successive editions of my *Theosophy* and see how I recast again and again the chapter on repeated earthly lives, for the very purpose of bringing the truth of this perception into relation with those ideas which are taken from observation of the sense world, will find what pains I took to do justice to the recognized scientific method.
>
> (*The Course of My Life*, pp. 329-30)

From these words it is evident how this chapter consciously appeals to the reader's ability to make more subtle observations of the sense world than is normally done. These observations provide the necessary basis for forming an idea of repeated earth lives. Only then does this idea lose its seemingly arbitrary character. In the course of the chapter Steiner guides the reader to consider more carefully than usual the nature of memory, how abilities arise out of experiences forgotten, the unique quality of every human biography, the similarities between "natural" gifts and faculties developed through practice, and so on.

Such observations awaken us to aspects of life which we normally overlook. They form the basis for new thoughts about the genesis and development of the human individuality. They can lead to the conclusion, as does this chapter, that "in each life the human spirit appears as a repetition of itself, with the fruits of its experiences in earlier lifetimes" (p. 81). Steiner's considerations are not, in the normal sense of the word, a "proof" of repeated earth lives. But they show that such thoughts can be arrived at when founded on discerning observation.

Why does Steiner take such pains to develop an idea that in the end appears only in its shadowy contours? In other contexts we find him describing very concretely and in great detail how the laws of reincarnation and karma work within human existence. But in this chapter he follows a specific intention:

> (The author) has pointed out that the conviction
> to which these thoughts lead is only sketchily

defined by them, that all they can do is prepare us in thought for what must ultimately be discovered by means of spiritual research. In itself, however, as long as this thought preparation does not exaggerate its own importance or attempt to prove anything, but only *trains our soul*, it entails an *inner effort* that can make us unbiased and receptive to facts we would simply take for foolish without it.

(Addendum, p. 91, italics added)

Steiner's intent is not to prove, it is to prepare and enable. He provides in the thought forms of this chapter a means for the soul to exercise its own faculties, faculties that will eventually lead to the certainty of reincarnation and karma out of one's own unmitigated experience.

V

Chapter 3 places the concepts of body, soul, and spirit into a much wider context. For just as the physical body can be understood only within the field of forces and substances of outer nature, so also must soul and spirit be considered in the context of their corresponding "environments." Steiner describes how, in the same sense that our physical body is not isolated within its own skin, independent of the natural world around it, neither does that which we know inwardly as the soul and spiritual aspects of our existence (see chapter 1) exist in isolation. They are part of a larger whole. The soul and spiritual worlds that Rudolf Steiner depicts do not, however, follow the laws of physics and biology as outer nature does. The "soul world" (*Seelenwelt*), as he describes it, is woven out of the interaction of two fundamental principles: sympathy and antipathy. Within the "country of spirit beings" (*Geisterland*), the spiritual archetypes, of which our ordinary thinking is but a shadow, are the creative law-giving elements.

Chapter 3 sets forth how these higher laws work within the development of the human being and shows their significance as constitutive elements within the kingdoms of nature.

Steiner is careful to note the difficulties involved in using language developed in reference to the sense-perceptible world to describe these levels of reality. Only with the help of similes and comparison is it possible to convey an impression of these "higher" worlds. This difficulty is apparent from the very beginning of this chapter—we see it in the use of the word "world." The soul and spiritual worlds Steiner describes are not to be pictured spatially, as being somewhere else, next to, or outside the physical. "These are *states of consciousness, not places.* One does not move from one location to the next when one moves through these regions" (*Grundbegriffe der Theosophie*, Nov. 7, 1904; italics added).

Thus, when Steiner speaks of journeys, of regions that are entered, we must keep characterizations such as the following in mind: "In physical space, . . . when we look down an avenue the distant trees appear, according to the laws of perspective, to stand closer together than those nearby. In soul space on the contrary, all objects appear at distances corresponding to their inner nature." This is not the space of "next to," or of "above and below." It is a qualitative "space" of inner relationship. A hint of such "soul space" comes to expression when we speak of being "close" to someone, or having grown inwardly "distant." To stretch our imagination beyond the familiar realm of three-dimensional experience is but one of the challenges this chapter presents.

Rudolf Steiner's descriptions of the soul world and spirit land, if taken seriously, shed tremendous light upon human existence. Nonetheless, for some readers they will appear to be unsupported pronouncements far from everyday life. Steiner recognized this possibility and described what was necessary to avoid it:

> [Someone] who has read the preceding discussions [chapters 1 and 2] only in order to take cognizance of the content, will find the truths set forth in these chapters [on the soul world and spirit land] to be mere assertions arbitrarily uttered. . . . [Anyone] who reads the first expositions in my book *Theosophy* without the impression of an inner experience, so that he or she does not become aware of a metamorphosis of his or her inner experience of ideas . . . can only arrive at a rejection of the book. But an anthroposophical book is designed to be taken up in inner experience. Then by stages a form of understanding comes about. This may be very weak, but it can — and should — exist. . . . A rightly composed

Anthroposophical book should be an *awakener* of
the life of the spirit in the reader, *not* a certain
quantity of *information* imparted. The reading of
it should be an experiencing with inner shocks,
tensions, solutions.

(*The Course of My Life*, p. 330; italics added)

VI

The issue of a "rightly composed Anthroposophical
book" has been an ongoing theme of this introduction. At
the beginning of the final chapter of *Theosophy* Rudolf
Steiner addresses just this matter. For here he describes
the path of knowledge, the way, namely, in which one at-
tains to the supersensible knowledge put forth in this
book. This path, he maintains, must take its starting point
from the realization that "thinking is the highest of the
faculties we human beings possess in the physical world"
(p. 176). This observation plays a central role in the work
of Rudolf Steiner. Throughout his life he addressed this
issue, shedding light upon it from the most varied perspectives. Already his first book, *The Science of Knowing*, written at the age of twenty five, contains a chapter
entitled "Thinking as a Higher Experience within Experience." There he observes:

With the rest of experience, if I stay with what
lies immediately before my senses, I cannot get
beyond the particulars. Assume that I have a liquid

which I bring to a boil. At first it is still; then I see bubbles rise; the liquid comes into movement and finally passes over into vapor form. Those are the successive individual perceptions. I can twist and turn the matter however I want: if I remain with what the senses provide, I find no connection between the facts. With thinking this is not the case. If, for example I grasp the thought "cause," this leads me by its own content to that of "effect." I need only hold onto the thoughts in the form in which they appear in direct experience and they manifest already as lawful characterizations.

What, for the rest of experience, must first be brought from somewhere else—if it is applicable to experience at all—namely, *lawful interconnection*, is already present in thinking in its very first appearance. ... *In thinking, what we must seek for with the rest of experience has itself become direct experience.*

(*The Science of Knowing*, p. 35-6)

Within the transparency of thinking we discover the laws of nature. The interrelationships between the phenomena of the sense world are not accessible to eyes and ears. (Otherwise the greatest scientists would simply be those with the best trained senses.) They first appear in thinking as a "higher experience within experience." Referring to the fact that our thinking life as such is not sense perceptible (he does not mean in this context our mental representations of the sense world), Steiner once spoke of a "pearl" contained therein, that normally remains unrecognized and thus undervalued.

> ...no one could *think* abstractly, could have thoughts and ideas if he or she were not clairvoyant. For in our ordinary thinking the *pearl of clairvoyance* is from the start contained. These thoughts and ideas arise in the soul through exactly the same process as that which gives rise to its highest powers. And it is immensely important to learn to understand that clairvoyance *begins* in something common and everyday. We only have to recognize the supersensible nature of our concepts and ideas. We must realize that these come to us from supersensible worlds; only then can we look at the matter rightly.
>
> (*The Occult Significance of the Bhagavad Gita*, lecture, May 29, 1913, pp. 25-6; italics added; see also T. Meyer, *Clairvoyance and Consciousness*, p. 54)

These supersensible worlds are the spiritual archetypes described in chapter 3. But, as Steiner points out there, our thoughts are merely a "shadowy picture" of their true reality in the supersensible world. In his book *Riddles of the Soul* Steiner describes how what we grasp in thinking loses its living reality as an active agency when it enters our consciousness as a concept. The transparent content (the pearl) remains, but its effectual reality is relinquished. This, as he further describes, has great significance, for if we were to experience our ideas in all their

dynamic vitality, we could never achieve individual freedom, nor self-consciousness. Existent forces, if they were
to enter our consciousness in this form, would compel.
Transparent thought semblances of these forces can not.
The latter we are free to accept in insight and to take up
as impulses for our own self-willed actions.[3] In a related
sense, Steiner also describes how we would never be able
to achieve self-consciousness if continually immersed in
the sea of forces which make up the actual substance of
the thought world.

It is Steiner's conviction that only on the *basis* of this
"abstract" thinking can true self-consciousness and freedom of the human will be attained. Nonetheless, if we are
to know the true nature of the human being we must
progress beyond this stage of consciousness, using it as a
healthy foundation for a deeper penetration into the realities of human existence. For this deeper penetration, our
thought life must gradually awaken to the living realities
out of which it originates.

Despite the "devitalized" nature of our normal concepts, Rudolf Steiner describes how this condition can be
overcome through the thought forms of spiritual science,
if they are taken up in the right way:

> Spiritual science puts in the place of finished
> concepts . . . something that the soul must repeat-
> edly work on anew; something that the soul must
> join with over and over again. If we have a good

---

3. See *The Tension between East and West*, lecture 1.

memory, we can receive the external truths as given to us by natural science once (and for all) and then possess them—because natural scientific truths are given in concepts that are, to a certain extent, dead. Natural laws, as concepts, are dead. Spiritual scientific concepts must be given in living concepts. If we condemn spiritual scientific truths to be dead concepts, if we take them in in the way we take in natural truths, then they are not food for the soul, but stones which cannot be digested.... This is certainly something about spiritual science that leaves many people unsatisfied, since they would like to have something finished.

(*Aspects of Human Evolution*, lecture, July 24, 1917; see also G. Kühlewind, *Working with Anthroposophy*, p. 74)

In this sense Rudolf Steiner sees the first step in the "path of knowledge" to be the active assimilation of spiritual scientific concepts. "Do not believe what I tell you, but think it"—that is his appeal to the reader. For these concepts are, he argues, seminal in nature, they are a means to awakening one's own consciousness to the living realities out of which not only our thought life, but ultimately the realms of nature around us come forth (see chapter 3). This is not a question of belief, Steiner maintains, but a matter of experience. Experience that gradually becomes accessible through the energetic application of one's thought forces to contents such as are those contained in this book.

But the enlivening of one's thinking is only one aspect of this path of development. The characterization of our thinking faculty as latent with higher capacities is also applicable to many aspects of the human being. How other human faculties can be consciously schooled so as to become organs of higher experience is the primary content of chapter 4. Already in the first pages of *Theosophy* a description of various "sides" of the human being was given, showing different ways in which we are connected with the world: through perception, feeling, will, and thinking. Whereas the first chapter remains primarily a description of these faculties, at the end of *Theosophy* they are viewed from a developmental perspective.

Although a healthy expansion of human consciousness begins with the faculty of thinking, it can only be realized at deeper levels when the "whole" human being is transformed. Chapter 4 shows the characteristic kinds of transformation the individual must undertake if he or she is to overcome the separation from the deeper aspects of reality created by the limitations of our "everyday" human qualities. This transformation, as Steiner describes it here, must be realized through the efforts of the human "I" itself. This core of our self-conscious being (see chapter 1) must take on this task through its own forces. Emphasizing this is essential in Steiner's view of the human being. The path of development which he represents does not happen "to" the human being, but is brought about through the growing forces of the individuality ("I") itself. Acting out of insight into the hindrances that it bears within its own bodily and soul nature, the human "I" can take upon itself a path of development which will enable it in time to overcome those limitations, transforming them lastly into organs of higher experience. This does not take place at the expense of the individuality, but through its enhancement.

VII

Does all this have relevance for the special difficulties we face at the end of the twentieth century? Can Rudolf Steiner's *Theosophy* help us to overcome the two cultures of which Snow spoke? Can it help us to free ourselves from the "paradigm rigidity" which threatens to splinter modern life into endless points of view? Can it, lastly, help us to find new ways to meet the concrete problems that modern society puts before us in ever greater number?

This would be a great deal to demand of one small book. In reality these questions would have to be addressed to Steiner's work as a whole—Anthroposophy. A careful study of the latter shows that Steiner did not bring a series of "ready-made" solutions for all of the challenges that face humanity today. What he did bring are deepened perspectives about the nature of the human being and the world of which it is a part. These perspectives lie hidden for the most part to the prevailing consciousness of our time. But they can be discovered by the conscientious pursuit of "higher" knowledge set forth in this book. Steiner's conviction is that by discovering the deeper wellsprings of our human existence, we will be able to heal in time the alienation that besets society today, to overcome those narrow perspectives that separate rather than unite. Such understanding can lead, lastly, as Rudolf Steiner himself was able to demonstrate in many realms of practical endeavor, to a renewal of human society down into the smallest details of "everyday" life.

Michael Holdrege

Before the ninth edition of this book was printed in 1918, I thoroughly revised and updated the text. This current edition has not been revised to the same extent, in spite of the fact that the publication of articles attacking the anthroposophical world-view this book presents has stepped up considerably since 1918. However, in the course of all my works, I make a practice of raising all foreseeable objections myself in order to be able to assess how serious they are and then refute them. Anyone who takes note of this will have a good idea of my response to these attacks. This time there was no intrinsic reason to make changes in the text as I had done in 1918, and although anthroposophy's worldview has certainly grown both broader and deeper within my soul during the last four years, this has not led to any earth-shattering changes in the book's content. On the contrary, what I have learned in the meantime suggests that I am justified in making no significant alterations to the content of this basic text.

Rudolf Steiner
Stuttgart
November 24, 1922

Once again, as I have done prior to the publication of several other editions of this book, I have reviewed the material presented in it, and the revisions for this ninth edition have expanded the content considerably. You will find that the chapter on reincarnation and karma has been almost completely reworked. I found no reason, however, to amend any of the results of spiritual scientific research presented in previous editions. Nothing significant has been omitted in this edition, but much has been added.

As a spiritual researcher, I constantly feel the need to shed new light on my subject from different angles in an attempt to make it ever clearer. In the preface to the sixth edition, I already mentioned feeling compelled to put my ongoing inner experience to optimum use in each nuance and turn of phrase. I have been especially aware of this obligation in preparing this new edition, which can therefore quite justifiably be called "thoroughly revised and updated."

Rudolf Steiner
Berlin
July 1918

PREFACE TO THE SIXTH EDITION

Almost every time it has become necessary to reprint this book, I have set myself the task of carefully reviewing and revising its contents. This time was no exception, but what I have to say about this new revision is similar to what I had to say about the third edition, so I will retain that Preface for this printing.

However, this time I have taken particular care to express many details with greater clarity than I had been capable of doing in any of the previous editions, although I realize that much remains to be done in this regard. In depicting the spiritual world, a researcher is dependent on the soul wending its own way toward the discovery of the pertinent word or appropriate phrase to express a fact or an experience. Somewhere along this way, at the right moment, this word or phrase, sought in vain when sought deliberately, simply appears. I believe that in many places in this new edition, I have been able to make a significant step in communicating details important for understanding the spiritual world. In fact, only now do some things seem to be presented as they should be. I must say that this volume has been part of my inner struggle for further knowledge of the spiritual world during the ten years since its first publication. Although the basic structure and even the wording of all crucial passages may be the same in this as in all earlier versions, it is noticeable at many junctures that I am now encountering my subject as a living thing, nourishing it on what I believe I have gained in ten years of challenging spiritual research. Of course it was necessary to keep all changes within quite modest limits if the book was to be simply a new edition of the old one rather than something totally new, but I made a particular effort to make sure that the Addenda would enable readers to find within the text itself the answers to many of the questions that might arise in the course of reading it.

These are agitated times, and my heart is moved as I write these lines prefacing this book's sixth edition. The printing had been completed up to page 192 when the destiny-laden events humanity is now experiencing broke in upon Europe. It did not seem right to write this Preface without acknowledging the storms breaking in upon our souls in times like these.

Rudolf Steiner
Berlin
September 7, 1914

What I said on the occasion of the second printing of this book applies equally to this third edition. This time, too, individual passages have been expanded and revised where I deemed it important for the sake of making aspects of the presentation more precise. However, I did not find it necessary to make any substantial changes in the content of the first and second editions, and nothing I said in the two earlier Prefaces with regard to the book's task and purpose needs to be revised at this time, so the Preface to the first edition, supplemented by the new material added in the Preface to the second, will serve as Preface for this edition as well:

Since the purpose of this book is to depict some portions of the supersensible world, anyone believing only in the validity of the sense-perceptible world will take it as a meaningless figment of the imagination. However, those interested in finding pathways leading out of the sense-perceptible world will soon realize that human life acquires value and meaning only through insight into another world. Many people are afraid that this insight might estrange them from "real life," but this fear is not justified.

On the contrary, this insight is the only way to learn to hold one's ground in ordinary life. It teaches us the causes underlying our life, while without it we would be groping our way blindly through the effects. It is only through knowledge of the supersensible that our sense-perceptible "reality" acquires meaning, and this knowledge makes people more fit for life rather than less so, since only someone who understands life can be truly practical.

In compiling this book, I have included nothing I cannot testify to on the basis of personal experience in this field. Only my direct experience is presented here.

This book cannot be read the way people ordinarily read books in this day and age. In some respects, its readers will have to work their way through each page and even each single sentence the hard way. This was done deliberately; it is the only way this book can become what it is intended to be for the reader. Simply reading it through is as good as not reading it at all. The spiritual scientific truths it contains must be experienced; that is the only way they can be of value.

This book cannot be assessed from the vantage point of current science unless the appropriate perspective has been acquired by means of the book itself. If its critics can adopt this point of view, they will realize that what is presented here is in no way contradictory to a truly scholarly and scientific approach. I am sure that I have set down nothing that would conflict with my own scientific scruples.

If a different way of seeking the truths presented here is wanted, one can be found in my Philosophy of Freedom. *These two books have the same goal but approach it differently. For understanding either of these books, the other one is by no means necessary, although some people may find it helpful.*

Some readers, hoping to find the "ultimate" truth in this book, may set it aside unsatisfied. However, its purpose is to present simply the most basic truths in the field of spiritual science. Of course, it is only human to immediately want to know how the world began and how it will end, to ask about the meaning of life and the nature of God. However, I am concerned not with mere words and concepts for people's rational understanding, but with truly viable knowledge, knowledge for life, and I know that certain things belonging to more advanced stages of wisdom may not be said in a book dealing with elementary levels of spiritual knowledge. Only through understanding these elementary stages can we learn how to ask questions of a higher sort. My book Occult Science *picks up where this book leaves off and contains more information on the subjects we will be discussing here.*

The Preface to the second edition included the following additional comments:

In this day and age, anyone presenting supersensible realities must be quite clear about two things: one, that the cultivation of supersensible knowledge is a necessity for our times; and two, that because of the kinds of thoughts and feelings pervading our culture, many people can only take any documentation of this sort to be the product of an imagination run wild. Supersensible knowledge is a necessity for our times because all the knowledge about life and the world that we acquire by ordinary means generates countless questions that can be answered only by means of supersensible truths. Let's not deceive ourselves—what present-day cultural trends can teach us about the basis of existence will never answer any of life's great riddles in the mind of a deeply feeling person; it will only raise questions. People may believe for a while that conclusions drawn from "strictly scientific data" or the deductions of some modern thinker or other will provide a solution to the riddles of life, but in the depths of soul where true self-knowledge becomes possible, what at first looked like a solution will only incite us to find the true question. And this question's answer should not simply satisfy our curiosity, for our inner equanimity and psychological integrity depend on it. It should not simply satisfy our thirst for knowledge, but should also make us fit to work and to face our tasks in life. On the other hand, if no answer to such questions is forthcoming, we become psychologically (and ultimately also physically) crippled. Supersensible knowledge is not a mere theoretical need; it is a matter of how we lead our practical life. And because of the state of our modern culture, knowledge of the spirit has become a field of study we cannot afford to ignore.

On the other hand, of course, what many people nowadays reject most emphatically is precisely what they most urgently need. The weight of opinion based on "irrefutable scientific results" is so overwhelming for many people that they cannot help thinking that a book like this contains nothing but blatant nonsense. However, it is quite possible for someone who can describe supersensible experiences to be free of any illusions while doing so. Of course people are tempted to insist that this person present "incontrovertible proof" of what he or she is talking about, but in succumbing to this temptation they succumb to an illusion as well. Without being aware of it, what they are demanding is not a proof intrinsic to the subject, but the kind of proof they themselves are willing and able to accept.

I know that I have written nothing in this book that anyone with a grounding in modern science would be unable to accept on that basis. I know that it is possible to fulfill all the requirements of science and yet apply that same background to recognizing that the method used here in describing the spiritual world is intrinsic to its subject. Anyone with a genuinely scientific way of thinking should feel quite at home in what I have to say, and will experience in many arguments to the contrary that, as Goethe so rightly put it, "A false teaching is not open to refutation because it rests on the conviction that what is false is true." It is pointless to enter into discussion with people who will accept only the validity of proofs that already lie within their personal mode of thought. But the mind has other ways of arriving at the truth than through arguing, as anyone aware of the essential nature of "proof" will know.

With this in mind, I offer the second edition of this book to the public.

Rudolf Steiner

*As an aid to readers wishing to follow the text in German,
the numbers that appear in the margins indicate
Rudolf Steiner's original paragraphing
in the German edition.*

In the autumn of 1813, the German philosopher Johann [1] Gottlieb Fichte published his *Science of Knowledge*, the mature fruit of a lifetime wholly dedicated to the service of truth. At the very beginning of this work, he wrote:

> This doctrine presupposes the existence of a quite new inner sensory instrument through which a new world is opened up, a world that simply does not exist for the ordinary person.

Fichte then showed by means of a comparison how incomprehensible this doctrine would be to anyone who insists on judging it on the basis of what our ordinary senses present:

> Imagine a world of people all born blind. They can only know about the existence and interrelationships of things that exist for the sense of touch. If you talk to them about colors and about other relationships that exist only through light and the

sense of sight, you might as well be saying nothing
at all. If you are lucky, they will inform you of this
fact so that you notice your error and can at least
refrain from further useless talk if you prove incapable of opening their eyes.[1]

All too often, someone trying to talk to people about
things such as those mentioned by Fichte is in a position
similar to that of a seeing person among the blind. Yet it is
precisely these things that are of relevance to the true nature and highest goals of human beings, and anyone who
really believed it necessary to "refrain from further useless
talk" would have to give up on humanity in despair. But
we must not doubt for a single moment that it is possible
to "open the eyes" of any person who responds to these
things with good will. This has always been the assumption of people who wrote and spoke out of feeling their
own "inner sensory instrument" maturing within them,
and were thus able to recognize the true nature of the human being, which is hidden from the outer senses. This is
why a "hidden wisdom" has been spoken of since time im-
memorial. Those who have grasped something of this hidden wisdom are as secure in their possession of it as people
with normal eyes are in their ability to visualize color;
thus, they need no "proof" of it. They also know that no

---

1. Johann Gottlieb Fichte, 1762-1814. From "Introductory Lectures
on the Theory of Science, Transcendental Logic and the Facts of
Consciousness," given at the University of Berlin, 1812-13. Published posthumously by I.H. Fichte in 1834.

proof is needed for anyone whose "higher sense," like their own, has been opened. They can speak to such a person just as a traveler might speak about a foreign country to people who have never been there personally, but who can imagine it because they would see the very same things, given the opportunity.

However, those capable of observing the supersensible world should speak not only to spiritual researchers but to everyone, since what they have to tell concerns each one of us. In fact, they know that without some knowledge of these things, no one can be human in the true sense of the word. They speak to all of us, knowing that what they have to say will be met with varying degrees of understanding, but also knowing that since a feeling for the truth and the ability to understand it are present in every human being, even those who are still far from being able to conduct spiritual research on their own may be able to respond with understanding. This understanding, which can light up in any healthy human soul, is what spiritual researchers address first, and they know that it has a power that must gradually lead to the higher stages of knowledge. This feeling for truth stirs in the darkness. Although it may at first see absolutely nothing of what is described, it is the magician who opens the "eye of the spirit." The soul does not yet see, but this feeling allows the power of truth to take hold of it, so that truth then gradually draws near the soul and opens its "higher sense." This may take more time or less, depending on the individual, but anyone with patience and perseverance will reach this goal. For although not every person born physically blind can be successfully

[2]

[3]   operated on, every spiritual eye can be opened; *when* it will be opened is simply a question of time.

Neither academic learning nor scientific training is a prerequisite for opening this higher sense; it can open up for a naive and uneducated person as readily as for a renowned scientist. In fact, what is nowadays often considered the one and only science is more likely to be a hindrance than a help on the way to this goal, because it characteristically accepts as "real" only what is accessible to our ordinary senses. However great the successes of science in understanding sense-perceptible reality may be, when it takes what is both necessary and beneficial in its own realm as the standard for all human knowledge, it creates a profusion of prejudices that block our access to higher realities.

[4]   The objection is often raised that human knowledge has been set "insurmountable limits," once and for all, which cannot be transcended, and any knowledge that disregards them must be rejected out of hand. Anyone who claims such knowledge is considered highly presumptous.This objection totally fails to take into account the fact that higher knowledge can come about only if a *development* of human cognitive powers precedes it. What lies outside the limits of human knowledge prior to this development lies well within them once the faculties that lie dormant in each individual have been awakened.

One point should not be overlooked, however. We could ask what good it does to talk to people about things for which their cognitive faculties are not yet awakened and that are therefore inaccessible to them. However, this is not the right way to look at the issue. We do need certain faculties in order to *discover* the kinds of things we are talking about, but if these ideas, once discovered, are shared and made known to others, they can be understood by anyone willing to apply impartial logic and a healthy feeling for the truth. To individuals who allow open, unbiased thinking and an unhampered, independent feeling for the truth to work freely within them, this book presents only things that offer a satisfying and convincing approach to the riddles of human life and the phenomena of the world around us. Ask yourselves this question: If the statements made in this book are true, do they offer a convincing explanation of life? You will find that the life of every human being offers confirmation that they do.

In order to be a "teacher" in these higher regions of existence, however, having acquired the faculty for perceiving them is not enough. Systematic knowledge belongs here as much as it does to the profession of teaching on the level of ordinary reality. "Higher seeing" does not make a person a "knower" in the spirit any more than healthy senses make a "scholar" in sense-perceptible reality. But in truth, *all* reality is one; since the lower reality and the higher spiritual reality are merely two sides of one and the same fundamental unity of being, a person who is ignorant with regard to lower knowledge will probably remain similarly ignorant of higher things. This basic fact calls up a feeling of boundless responsibility in those who, through a spiritual calling, feel obliged to speak out about spiritual regions of existence. It impresses on them the need for humility and restraint. It

[5]

should not, however, discourage anyone from looking into higher truths, not even someone whose everyday life offers no opportunity to study the ordinary sciences. It is quite possible to fulfill our tasks as human beings without understanding anything about botany, zoology, mathematics or other sciences, but it is not possible to be "human" in the fullest sense of the word without coming closer in some way to the essential nature and destiny of the human being as revealed through knowledge of the supersensible world.

[6]   As human beings we call the highest thing we can look up to "the Divine," and we must imagine that our highest aim and calling have something to do with this divine element. This may well be why wisdom that transcends the sense-perceptible world, that reveals to us both our essential nature and our destiny, is called *theosophy*, or "divine wisdom." The name "spiritual science" can be given to the observation of spiritual processes in human life and in the cosmos. If, as has been done in this book, we extract from spiritual science the phenomena pertaining especially to the essential spiritual core of the human being, then we can use the term "theosophy" for this particular subject area, since it has been applied in this sense for centuries.

[7]   The above viewpoint provided the basis for developing this outline of the theosophical worldview. Its author has included nothing that is not fact and reality for him in the same sense that events in the outer world are facts and realities for our eyes, ears and ordinary understanding. Here, we are dealing with experiences that become accessible to

anyone determined to set off on the path to knowledge described in the last chapter of this book. We approach the things of the supersensible world with the right attitude if we take it as a given that sound thinking and perception are capable of understanding all true knowledge that can flow toward us from the higher worlds. We should also recognize that by taking this kind of understanding as our starting point and laying a firm foundation with it, we are taking a great and important first step toward higher seeing for ourselves, although other things must also contribute if we are to achieve this goal. However, if we scorn this approach and try to reach the higher worlds by other means alone, we bar the door to true higher knowledge. If, on principle we admit the existence of higher worlds only once we have seen them for ourselves, this in itself is an obstacle to ever being able to see them, but being determined to use sound thinking to understand first what we will later be able to observe actually fosters this seeing. It summons up important forces of the soul that lead to this seership.

CHAPTER 1

THE
ESSENTIAL NATURE
OF THE HUMAN BEING

The following words by Goethe beautifully characterize   *[1]*
the starting point of one of the paths that lead to being able
to recognize the true nature of the human being:

> As soon as we become aware of the objects
> around us, we start to consider them in relationship
> to ourselves, and rightly so, because our fate de-
> pends entirely on whether they please or displease,
> attract or repel, help or harm us. This very natural
> way of looking at and assessing things appears to be
> as easy as it is necessary, yet it exposes us to thou-
> sands of errors that often put us to shame and make
> our lives miserable.
>
> We undertake a much harder task when, in our
> keen desire for knowledge, we strive to observe nat-
> ural objects in and for themselves and in their rela-
> tionship to one another, for we soon feel the lack of
> the standard of liking and disliking, attraction and

repulsion, usefulness and harmfulness, that came to our aid when we were considering objects in relationship to our human selves. We are forced to renounce this standard totally and, as dispassionate and quasi-divine beings, to seek out and examine what *is*, and not what pleases us. This means that neither the beauty nor the usefulness of any plant should move true botanists, who rather should study its morphology and its relationships to the rest of the plant kingdom. Just as the sun shines equally on all plants and entices them forth, so too should botanists observe and survey them all impartially and take the data and standards for their assessment, not from the human domain, but from the domain of the things under observation.[1]

[2]   Goethe's thoughts draw our attention to three different kinds of things: first, the objects we constantly receive information about through the gateways of our senses, the things we touch, taste, smell, hear and see; second, the impressions they make on us, which assume the character of liking or disliking, desire or disgust, by virtue of the fact that we react sympathetically to one thing and are repelled by another, or find one thing useful and another

1. Johann Wolfgang von Goethe, 1749-1832, German poet, dramatist, novelist, and scientist. From Goethe's treatise *Der Versuch als Vermittler von Object und Subject*, "The Experiment as Mediator between Object and Subject," 1793. (*Scientific Studies: Johann Wolfgang Goethe*, ed. and trans. Douglas Miller, New York: Suhrkamp Publishers, 1988.)

harmful; and third, the knowledge we "quasi-divine be-ings" acquire about the objects as they tell us the secrets of what they are and how they work.

These three domains are distinctly separate in human life, so we become aware that we are bound up with the world in three different ways. The first way is something we encounter and accept as a given fact; through the second way, we turn the world into something that concerns us and has significance for us; the third way we hold as a goal to strive for unceasingly. *[3]*

Why does the world appear to us in this threefold man-ner? A simple example can make it clear. Suppose I walk through a field where wildflowers are blooming. The flowers reveal their colors to me through my eyes—that is the fact I accept as given. When I then take pleasure in the wonderful display of colors, I am turning the fact into something that concerns me personally—that is, by means of my feelings, I relate the flowers to my own existence. A year later, when I go back to the same field, new flowers are there and they arouse new joy in me. The previous year's enjoyment rises up as a memory; it is present in me although the object that prompted it in the first place is gone. And yet the flowers I am now seeing are of the same species as last year's and have grown in accordance with the same laws. If I am familiar with this species and these laws, I will recognize them again in this year's flowers, just as I did in last year's. On reflection, I may realize that since last year's flowers are gone, my enjoyment of them remains only in my memory; it is bound up with my per-sonal existence alone. But what I recognized in the flowers *[4]* both last year and this year will remain as long as such flowers grow; it is something that is revealed to me but is not dependent on my existence in the same way that my enjoyment is. My feelings of pleasure remain within me, while the laws, the essence of the flowers, exist in the world outside of me.

[5]   Thus, as human beings, we are constantly linking ourselves to the things of the world in a threefold way. (We should not read anything into this fact at first, but simply take it as it stands.) It shows us that there are three aspects to our human nature. For the moment, this and only this is what will be meant here by the three terms *body, soul* and *spirit.* Associating any preconceived ideas or even hypotheses with these words will cause us to misunderstand the discussion that follows. By *body* is meant the means by which the things in our environment, such as the wildflowers in the example above, reveal themselves to us. The word *soul* designates the means by which we link these things to our own personal existence, by which we experience likes and dislikes, pleasure and displeasure, joy and sorrow. By *spirit* is meant what becomes apparent in us when, as "quasi-divine beings," to use Goethe's expression, we look at the things of the world. In this sense, each person consists of *body, soul and spirit.*

[6]   Through the body, we are capable of linking ourselves for the moment to things outside us. Through the soul, we preserve the impressions things make on us. Through the spirit, what the things themselves contain is disclosed to us. Only when we look at the human being from these

three sides can we hope to understand our true nature, for these three sides show us that we are related to the rest of the world in a threefold way.

Through the body, we are related to the things that [7] present themselves to our senses from outside. The substances of the outer world make up the body, and the forces of the outer world are active in it. We can observe our own bodily existence with our senses, just as we observe the things of the outside world, but it is not possible to observe our soul existence in the same way. With my bodily senses, I can observe the whole range of bodily processes taking place in me, but neither I nor anyone else can perceive my likes and dislikes or my joys and sorrows with bodily senses. The domain of the soul is inaccessible to bodily perception. Our bodily existence is there for all to see, but we carry our soul existence inside us as our own private world. Through the spirit, however, the outer world is revealed to us in a higher way. Although it is true that the secrets of the outer world disclose themselves inside us, in the spirit we step outside of ourselves and let the things themselves tell us what is significant for them, rather than for us. When we look up at the starry sky, the soul's experience of delight belongs to us, but the eternal laws of the stars, which we may grasp in thought and in spirit, do not belong to us. They belong to the stars.

Thus as human beings we are citizens of three worlds. [8] In body, we both belong to and perceive the outer world; in soul, we build up our own inner world; and in spirit, a third world that is higher than both of the others reveals itself to us.

[9]   It should be apparent that, because of the fundamental differences between these three worlds, we will achieve a clear understanding of them and of our own part in them only by applying three different modes of observation.

I. The Bodily Nature of the Human Being

[10]   We learn about the human body by means of our bodily senses, and our mode of observation can be no different than if we were learning about other sense-perceptible things. We can observe the human being in the same way that we observe minerals, plants and animals, and as human beings, we are related to these three other forms of existence. Like the minerals, we build up our bodies out of natural substances; like the plants, we grow and reproduce; like the animals, we perceive the objects around us and develop inner experiences based on the impressions they make on us. Therefore, we may attribute a mineral, a plant and an animal existence to the human being.

[11]   The structural differences between minerals, plants and animals correspond to their three modes of existence. Their structure or *Gestalt* (form) is what we can perceive with our senses, and this alone is what may be called "the body." The human body, however, is different from the animal body. We all recognize this difference, no matter what we may think about how humans are related to animals. Even the most radical materialist, who denies the existence of anything having to do with the soul, would be hard put to disagree with the following statement by

Carus in his *Organon of the Knowledge of Nature and the Spirit*:

Even though the most delicate inner construction of the nervous system and especially of the brain remains an unsolved riddle for physiologists and anatomists, it is an undisputed fact that the concentration of its structures increases in the higher orders of animals, reaching in the human being a level not to be found in any other creature. This fact, of the greatest significance with regard to human intellectual development, may in itself be sufficient to explain that development. Therefore, when the structure of the brain has not developed properly and shows itself to be small and inadequate as is the case in microcephalics and idiots, it goes without saying that we can no more expect to find understanding and the appearance of original ideas than we can expect the continuation of the species to be accomplished by individuals with totally deformed reproductive organs. In contrast, although it may not in itself guarantee genius, the strong and beautifully developed structure of the whole person and of the brain in particular is at least the first and indispensable prerequisite of higher knowledge.[2]

---

2. Carl Gustav Carus, 1789-1869, German naturalist, physician, psychologist and landscape painter. From the chapter "On Knowledge" in *Organon der Erkenntnis der Natur und des Geistes* ["Organon of the Knowledge of Nature and the Spirit"], Leipzig, 1856, p. 89ff.

[12]   Just as we attribute mineral, plant and animal modes of existence to the human body, we must also attribute to it a fourth and distinctively human mode. Through the mineral mode of existence we are related to everything visible, through the plant-like mode to everything that grows and reproduces, and through the animal mode to all creatures that perceive their environment and have inner experiences based on outer impressions. But through the human mode, even with regard to the physical body, we make up a kingdom that is ours alone.

II. The Soul Nature of the Human Being

[13]   As an individual private inner world, soul nature is different from bodily nature. Its intrinsic privateness becomes apparent as soon as we turn our attention to the simplest act of sensing. We cannot know whether or not others experience this simple sensation in exactly the same way. We know that some people are color-blind and experience things only in different shades of gray, while others are partially color-blind and cannot perceive certain gradations of color. The image of the world that their eyes provide is different from that of a so-called normal person. The same applies to the other senses, too, more or less. This is already enough to demonstrate that even a simple sensation belongs to the private inner world. With my bodily senses, I can perceive the same red table that someone else perceives, but I cannot perceive that person's sensation of red. Therefore,

we must describe this sensation as belonging to the soul. Once we are quite clear about this, we will stop looking at inner experiences as mere brain processes or something of that sort.

Feeling follows closely on sensation, with one sensation arousing pleasure in us and another displeasure. These are the stirrings of our inner soul life. We each create an inner world of feelings in addition to the world that works in on us from outside. Then there is a third factor, our will, through which we work back upon the outside world, leaving the imprint of our own inner being on it. In will activity, the soul flows outward, in a sense. The fact that our actions bear the stamp of our inner life distinguishes them from natural events taking place in the outer world. In this way the soul sets itself up as something personal and private in contrast to the world outside. It receives stimuli from the outer world, but constructs an inner private world in accordance with them. Bodily existence becomes the basis for soul existence.

III. The Spirit Nature of the Human Being

The soul element in a human being is not determined exclusively by the body. We do not wander aimlessly and without direction from one sense impression to another, nor do we respond to every random stimulus that acts on us from outside or through our bodily processes. Instead, we think about our sensations and our actions. By thinking about our sensations, we come to an understanding of

[14]

things; by thinking about our actions, we create a rational coherence in our lives. And we know that we are only worthily fulfilling our tasks as human beings when we let ourselves be guided by the right thoughts, both in knowing and in acting. Therefore, the human soul faces a dual necessity. Out of natural necessity, it is governed by the laws of the body, but because it freely recognizes their necessity it also allows itself to be governed by the laws that lead to correct thinking. Nature subjects us to the laws of metabolism, but as human beings we subject ourselves to the laws of thought.

Through this process, we make ourselves members of a higher order than the one we belong to through the body. This is the spiritual order. Soul is different from spirit, as different as it is from the body. As long as we simply speak of the particles of carbon, hydrogen, oxygen and nitrogen moving around in our body, we do not have the soul in view. The life of the soul begins only at the point where sensation arises within such movement, where we taste something sweet or feel pleasure. In the same way, we do not have the spirit in view as long as we consider only the inner experiences that pass through us when we give ourselves completely to the outer world and to the life of the body. Rather, this soul existence is the basis for the spiritual, just as bodily existence is the basis for soul existence. The natural scientist (biologist) deals with the body, the soul scientist (psychologist) with the soul, and the spiritual scientist with the spirit. Anyone trying to understand the essential nature of the human being by means of thinking is first required to come, through self-reflection, to a clear understanding of the difference between body, soul and spirit.

IV. Body, Soul, and Spirit

The only valid way for us to shed light on ourselves as human beings is by clearly grasping the significance of thinking within our overall being. The bodily instrument of thinking is the brain. We can see colors only by means of a well-formed eye; similarly, only an appropriately constructed brain can serve the purpose of thinking. The whole human body is built up in such a way that the brain, the organ of the spirit, is its crowning glory. We can understand the structure of the human brain only when we look at it in relationship to its function, which is to serve as the bodily basis for the thinking spirit. This is demonstrated by a comparative survey of the animal kingdom: In amphibians the brain is relatively small in proportion to the spinal cord, in mammals it is larger, and in humans it is largest of all in proportion to the rest of the body. [15]

Numerous prejudices prevail against observations about thinking such as those being made here. Many people tend to underestimate thinking and to place more value on the warmth and depth of feelings or sensations. They even claim that it is not through sober thinking but through the warmth of feelings, through the direct power of sensations, that we ascend to higher knowledge. These people are afraid that clear thinking will deaden their feelings. This is certainly true of mundane thinking that is [16] concerned only with utilitarian things, but exactly the opposite is true of thoughts that lead to higher levels of existence. No feeling and no enthusiasm on earth can compare with the sensations of warmth, beauty and exaltation that are enkindled by pure, crystal-clear thoughts relating to higher worlds. Our loftiest feelings are not the ones that happen by themselves, but the ones achieved through strenuous and energetic thinking.

[17]   The human body is built up in such a way that it meets the requirements of thinking; that is, the same substances and forces that are also present in the mineral kingdom are put together in the human body in a way that allows thinking to appear. For purposes of the following discussion, we will call this mineral structure, formed in accordance with its function, "the physical body" of the human being.

[18]   This mineral structure, organized with the brain as its center, comes about through reproduction and achieves its mature form through growth. Reproduction and growth are characteristics that human beings have in common with plants and animals; they distinguish a living being from a lifeless mineral. Living things develop out of other living things by means of the reproductive cells; descendants are linked to their ancestors in the succession of generations. The forces through which a mineral comes into being are directed toward the substances composing it—a quartz crystal takes shape through forces inherent in the silicon and oxygen combined in it. But the forces that shape an oak tree must be looked for indirectly in the reproductive cells of the parent plants. Through reproduction, the form

of the oak is maintained and passed on from ancestor to descendant in accordance with the inner, inborn dictates of life. People had a crude view of nature indeed when they believed that lower animals and even fish could take shape out of mud. A living being's form is reproduced through heredity, and how it develops depends on the parents it came from, or, in other words, on the species it belongs to. The substances that make it up are continually changing, but its species remains constant throughout its lifetime and is passed on to its descendants through heredity. The species is therefore what determines how the substances are put together. We will call the species-determining force the life force.[3] Just as mineral forces express themselves in crystals, the formative life force expresses itself in the species, or forms, of plant and animal life.

As human beings, we perceive mineral forces by means   *[19]*
of our bodily senses. We can only perceive things for which we possess the corresponding bodily sense. Without

---

3. Not too long ago any mention of a "life force" or "vital force" was taken as an indication of an unscientific mind. Here and there, however, we now begin to meet scientists who are no longer opposed to the idea of a vital force as it was understood in times past. But if we examine the progress of modern scientific thought, we find that those who refuse to acknowledge the existence of a vital force are more consistent in their logic, and it is certainly true that this life force does not belong to what we currently call "the forces of nature." In fact, anyone who is unwilling to dispense with modern science's habitual concepts and ways of thinking and to make the step to a higher mode of thinking should refrain from using the term at all. Only spiritual scientific presuppositions and a spiritual scientific way of thinking make it possible to approach such things without being self-contradictory.

the eye there would be no perception of light, without the ear no perception of sound. Of those senses present in human beings, only a kind of sense of touch is possessed by the very lowest organisms; for them, only the mineral forces perceptible to this sense are perceived in the way human senses perceive them.[4] The degree to which the

---

3. *(continued)* Current theorists who are attempting to come to purely scientific conclusions have abandoned the belief (prevalent in the second half of the nineteenth century) that the phenomena of life can be explained solely in terms of forces that are also at work in inanimate nature. Noted naturalist Oskar Hertwig's book refuting the Darwinian theory of chance is a scientific phenomenon that sheds light far and near. (Oskar Hertwig, 1849-1922, zoologist; professor in Berlin from 1888-1921. The book referred to is *Das Werden der Organismen. Eine Widerlegung von Darwins Zufallstheorie* [*The Development of Organisms: A Refutation of Darwin's Theory of Chance*]).It challenges the assumption that the interworking of mere physical and chemical laws is sufficient to give rise to life. Also significant is the so-called neovitalist viewpoint which, like the older "vital force" theory, admits the possibility of forces unique to life. However, we cannot get beyond abstract schematic concepts in this field unless we recognize that to grasp the aspect of life that transcends the activity of inorganic forces, we must use a mode of perception that rises to supersensible vision. When we enter the realm of life, it is not enough simply to continue to apply the methods of understanding we have always applied to the inorganic world. A whole new way of knowing is needed.

4. Here, the "sense of touch" of lower organisms is not the same thing as what the term usually means in descriptions of the "senses," and in fact, from the point of view of spiritual science, a lot can be said against the use of the term in this context. In this case, "sense of touch" means becoming generally aware of an impression coming from outside, as opposed to acquiring a specific awareness that consists in seeing, hearing, and so on.

other senses of higher animals have developed determines the richness and variety of their surroundings for them, the surroundings that human beings also perceive. Therefore, the organs that a living being possesses determine whether or not something present in the environment is also present for it as a perception or a sensation. For instance, what is present in the air as a certain kind of movement becomes the sensation of sound for human beings.

We do not perceive the manifestations of the life force by means of our ordinary senses. We see the colors of plants and smell their fragrance, but the life force is concealed from this kind of observation. However, our ordinary senses have as little right to deny the existence of the life force as a person born blind has to deny the existence of colors. Colors are present for a blind person after a successful eye operation, and in the same way the plant and animal species—not just the individual plants and animals—created by the life force are also present for those whose corresponding organ has opened up. A whole new world is disclosed to us once this organ has opened. From that point on, we perceive not only the colors, scents and so forth of living things, we perceive their very life itself. In every plant and animal, we perceive the life-filled spiritual form in addition to the physical form. Since we need a name for this spirit form, we will call it the ether body or life body.

For investigators of spiritual life, the ether body is not merely a result of the physical body's substances and forces, but a real, independent entity that calls these same substances and forces to life. Speaking in the sense of spiritual science, we might put it like this: A body that is merely material—for example, a crystal—owes its form to the physical formative forces inherent in lifeless matter; a living body, however, cannot owe its form to these same forces, since it starts to decay immediately once life has abandoned it and it has been surrendered to physical forces alone.[5] The life body is present at every moment of

---

5. For a long time after compiling this book, I also spoke of what is here termed "ether body" or "life body" as "the body of formative forces." I felt compelled to give it this name because I believed one could not do enough to try to prevent the identification of what I meant with the "life force" or "vital force" of an earlier stage of science. When it comes to refuting this outdated concept, as modern science does, I agree in some respects with those who would deny the existence of any such force. That term was used in an attempt to explain the unique way of working that inorganic forces took on within a living organism. However, inorganic activity is actually no different inside an organism than it is outside in inorganic nature. Within an organism there is simply something additional present, something that is not inorganic, namely the formative activity of life whose basis is the ether body or body of formative forces. Recognizing the existence of the ether body in no way impinges on the legitimate task of science, which is to trace the effects of forces observed in inorganic nature into the world of living organisms. Spiritual science, however, also finds it justified not to imagine these effects as altered by a particular "vital force" within an organism. A spiritual researcher speaks of an ether body at the point where an organism discloses something that a lifeless object cannot.

In spite of all this, I do not find it necessary to replace the term "ether body" with "body of formative forces" in this book, since in this context anyone who so chooses will be able to avoid misunderstanding. Misunderstanding will only arise if this term is used in an incompatible context.

life as an entity that constantly maintains the physical body against decay. In order to see this life body, to perceive it in another living being, we need the awakened spiritual eye. We may be able to deduce the existence of the ether body on logical grounds without this spiritual eye, but we can "see" it with the spiritual eye, just as we see colors with the physical eye. Please do not take offense at the term "ether body," but take it simply as a name for what is described here. "Ether" as the word is used here means something different from the hypothetical ether of nineteenth-century physics.

In its structure, the human ether body, like the human physical body, is an image of its function. It too can be understood only in relation to the thinking spirit. The human ether body differs from that of plants and animals in being organized to support the thinking spirit. Just as we belong to the mineral world through our physical body, we belong to the world of life through our ether body. After death, the physical body disintegrates into the mineral world, the ether body into the world of life. The term "body" is used here to designate what gives a being of any kind its form, shape or *Gestalt*. It should not be confused with the sense-perceptible form of the material body. As used in this book, the term "body" can also refer to something that takes on form in soul or in spirit.

The life body is still something external to us, but with [20] the first stirrings of sensation our inner self responds to the stimuli of the outer world. No matter how far we pursue what we justifiably call the "external world," we will never be able to find sensation. Rays of light penetrate into the eye, to the retina, where they stimulate chemical changes in what is called the visual purple in the rods of the retina. The effect of this stimulus then moves along the visual nerve to the brain, where further physical processes take place. If we could actually observe this happening, we would simply see physical processes like those that take place anywhere else in the external world. But if we are able to observe the ether body, we will perceive how a physical process taking place in the brain is also a life process. However, the sensation of the blue color that the recipient of the light rays experiences is still nowhere to be found; it only comes about in the recipient's soul. If the recipient's constitution consisted only of the physical body and the ether body, sensation could not take place. The activity through which sensation becomes a fact fundamentally differs from the working of the formative life force and elicits from it an inner experience. Without this activity, our response to external stimuli would be nothing more than a mere life process such as those we observe in plants. Picture human beings receiving impressions from all sides. Our sensations respond to all these impressions, so we also picture ourselves as the source of the sentient activity described above, which moves out in all the directions from which we receive impressions. We will call this source of activity the sentient soul. It is just as real as the physical body. If a person stands before me and I disregard his or her sentient soul, imagining that person merely as a physical body, it is as if I were imagining a painting as nothing more than its canvas.

With regard to perceiving the sentient soul, we must [21] say something similar to what was said earlier about the ether body. Our bodily organs are blind to the sentient soul, and so is the organ by which life can be perceived as life, by which the ether body can be perceived. But by means of a still higher organ, the inner world of sensations can become a particular kind of supersensible perception. As we develop this organ, we become able not only to sense the impressions of the physical and ether worlds, but also to see the sensations as such. At that point, another being's world of sensations is spread out before us like any outer reality. We must differentiate between experiencing our own world of sensations and perceiving that of someone else—of course anyone can look into his or her own personal world of sensations, but only a seer with an opened "spiritual eye" can see the inner sensations of another being. Unless we are seers, we can know the world of sensation only as something within ourselves, as the personal and hidden experiences of our own souls, but when our "spiritual eye" is open, what otherwise lives hidden inside another being shines forth, accessible to our outward-looking spiritual gaze.

To avoid misunderstanding, it should be expressly stat- [22] ed that a seer does not inwardly experience the content of the inner worlds of sensations belonging to other beings. These beings experience their perceptions and sensations from their own inner points of view, while the seer perceives a manifestation or expression of each one's world of sensations.

[23]   In its functioning, the sentient soul is dependent on the
ether body, because it draws from the ether body what it
then allows to light up as sensation. And since the ether
body is the life within the physical body, the sentient soul
is indirectly dependent on the physical body as well. Only
a properly functioning and well-formed eye makes accurate color sensations possible. This is how the bodily nature affects the sentient soul. The sentient soul is thus
determined and restricted in its activity by the physical
body, and lives within the limits set by our bodily nature.
That is, the physical body, which is built up out of mineral
substances and enlivened by the ether body, in turn sets
the limits for our sentient soul. Those who possess the
above-mentioned organ for "seeing" the sentient soul
therefore recognize it as having limits set by the body.

However, the boundaries of the sentient soul do not coincide with those of the material physical body. The sentient soul extends beyond the physical body, even though
the force that determines its limits proceeds from the
physical body. This means that still another distinct member of the human constitution inserts itself between the
physical and ether bodies on the one hand and the sentient
soul on the other. This is the sentient or soul body. To say
it another way, a portion of the ether body is finer than the
rest, and this finer part forms a unity with the sentient
soul, while the coarser part forms a kind of unity with the
physical body. However, the sentient soul extends beyond the soul body.

[24]   For simplicity sake, we have chosen the term "sentient
soul," which is related to "sensing." But in fact, "sensing"

is only one aspect of the soul's being. Our feelings of pleasure and displeasure, our drives, instincts and passions, are all very close to our sensations. They are all similarly private and individual in character and similarly dependent on our bodily nature.

• • •

Our sentient soul interacts with thinking, with the spirit, [25] just as it does with the body. To begin with, thinking serves the sentient soul: we formulate thoughts about our sensations and thus explain the outer world to ourselves. For instance, a child who has been burned thinks about it and arrives at the conclusion that fire burns. We do not blindly pursue our drives, instincts and passions; we think about them, thus creating opportunities to gratify them. This is the direction taken by our material culture, which is the sum of the services rendered to the sentient soul by thinking. Vast amounts of thoughtpower are directed toward this end. Thoughtpower has created ships, railroads, telegraphs and telephones—all things that for the most part serve to satisfy the needs of sentient souls.

We have seen how the formative life force pervades the physical body. In a similar way, thoughtpower pervades the sentient soul. The formative life force connects the physical body to its ancestors and descendants and thus places it in the context of natural laws having nothing to do with mere minerals. Similarly, thoughtpower gives the soul a place within a system of laws to which it does not belong as mere sentient soul.

Through the sentient soul, we are related to the animals, in whom we can also recognize the presence of sensations, drives, instincts and passions. Animals, however, follow these up directly without interweaving them with independent thoughts that transcend immediate experience.[6] This is also the case to a certain extent with less developed human beings. As such, therefore, the sentient soul is different from the more highly evolved part of the soul that places thinking in its service. We may call this soul, which is served by thinking, the mind soul.

---

6. Spiritual scientific statements must be taken very exactly, because they are of value only if the ideas are expressed precisely. For example, take the sentence, "...animals follow these [perceptions, instincts, etc.] up directly without interweaving them with independent thoughts that go beyond their immediate experience...." If the modifiers "independent" and "that go beyond their immediate experience" are not fully taken into account, it would be easy to make the mistake of assuming that what is meant here is that no thoughts are present in the sensations and instincts of animals. However, true spiritual science is based on the recognition that the inner experience of animals, like everything else in existence, is permeated with thoughts, although these thoughts are not those of an independent "I" living within each animal. Instead, they belong to a collective animal ego that must be seen as a being that governs the individual animals from outside. This collective ego, unlike the human "I," is not present in the physical world but works on the animals from the soul world described on pp. 93ff. (Further details may be found in *An Outline of Occult Science* by this author.) The point here is that in human beings, thoughts acquire an independent existence; that is, we can have a direct soul experience of them as thoughts rather than experiencing them indirectly in sensation.

The mind soul permeates the sentient soul. Anyone   *[26]*
who possesses the organ for "seeing" the soul will see the
mind soul as an entity distinct from the mere sentient
soul.[7]

* * *

Through thinking, we are led beyond our own personal   *[27]*
lives; we acquire something that extends beyond our
own souls. We take it as a matter of course that the laws
of thinking correspond with the universal order. We can
feel at home in the universe because this correspondence
exists, and it is a weighty factor in learning to recognize
our own essential nature. We seek the truth in our soul;
through this truth, not only the soul but also the things of
the world express themselves. Truth recognized through
thinking has an independent significance, which refers to
the things of the world and not merely to our own souls.
In my delight in the starry heavens, I am living inside
myself, but the thoughts that I formulate about the orbits
of the heavenly bodies have the same meaning for anyone else's thinking as they have for mine. It would be

---

7. Translator's note: It is important to note that Rudolf Steiner here
uses both the terms *Verstandesseele* (mind soul or rational soul) and
Gemütsseele, "heart-and-mind soul," even equating *Verstandesseele*
with that untranslatable German concept, *Gemüt*. In this context, the
relationship of the mind-soul to *Gemüt* even in its non-anthropo-
sophical usage (warm-heartedness, kindly disposition), as well as to
Gemütlichkeit (comfort, coziness) is apparent.

senseless to speak of "my" delight and pleasure if I my-self were not present, but it is not at all senseless to talk about my thoughts without reference to me as a person. The truth I think today was also true yesterday and will be true tomorrow, even though it occupies my mind only for today. If understanding something gives me plea-sure, this pleasure is meaningful only as long as it is ac-tive in me, but the truth of the understanding has a significance totally independent of my pleasure. In grasping the truth, the soul links up with something that possesses intrinsic value, a value that neither appears nor disappears with the soul's perception of it. The real truth neither comes into being nor passes away; its signifi-cance cannot be destroyed.

This is in no way contradicted by the fact that certain human "truths" are of only temporary value because they are recognized as partial or total errors in due time. We must realize that the truth, in itself, endures, even though our thoughts are only transient manifestations of eternal truths. Even if, like Lessing, we say that we are content to strive eternally for the truth since the pure and perfect truth can surely exist only for a god, this does not deny the eternal value of the truth, but rather confirms it.[8] Only something of eternal and intrinsic significance can evoke an eternal striving and be the object of an eternal search. If the truth were not wholly independent in itself, if its value and significance came from the feelings of human souls, then it could not be a goal agreed on by all

8. Gotthold Ephraim Lessing, 1729-1781, German dramatist and critic.

humankind. The very fact that we all strive for it confirms its independent nature.

This applies equally to what is truly good. What is morally right is independent of our inclinations and passions insofar as it does not submit to them but makes them submit to it. Desire and revulsion, likes and dislikes, are the property of each individual human soul, but duty stands higher than likes and dislikes, sometimes standing so high in people's estimation that they will give up their lives for it. The more we have ennobled our inclinations, our likes and dislikes, so that they submit without force or compulsion to what we recognize as our duty, the higher we stand as human beings. What is morally right, like what is true, has an intrinsic eternal value that it does not receive from the sentient soul.

[28]

By letting what is intrinsically true and good come to life within us, we rise above the mere sentient soul. The eternal spirit shines into the sentient soul, kindling in it a light that will never go out. To the extent that our soul lives in this light, it takes part in something eternal, which it links to its own existence. What the soul carries within itself as truth and goodness is immortal. We will call this eternal element that lights up within the soul the consciousness soul.

[29]

We can speak of consciousness even in connection with the soul's lower stirrings; even the most mundane sensation is already the object of consciousness, and to this extent animals must also be credited with having consciousness. But the very core of human consciousness, the "soul within the soul," so to speak, is what "consciousness soul" means here. The consciousness soul is different from the mind soul, which is still entangled in sensations, drives, emotions and so forth. We all know how we accept our personal preferences as true, at first. But truth is lasting only when it has freed itself from any flavor of such sympathies and antipathies. The truth is true, even if all our personal feelings revolt against it. We will apply the term "consciousness soul" to that part of the soul in which truth lives.

[30]   Thus the soul, like the body, consists of three distinct members—the sentient soul, the mind soul, and the consciousness soul. Just as our bodily nature works from below upwards to set limits on the soul, spirituality works from above downwards to expand it. The more our soul is filled with what is true and good, the broader and more inclusive its eternal aspect becomes.

For anyone who can "see" the soul, the glow that proceeds from a human being whose eternal aspect is expanding is as real as a flame's radiant light is to the physical eye. To the seer, the visible bodily person is only a part of the whole human being, the coarsest structure in the midst of others that interpenetrate it and each other. The ether body as a life form fills out the physical body, and beyond the ether body we can distinguish the soul body or astral form projecting outward on all sides. Extending beyond this is the sentient soul, and then the mind soul that grows ever larger as it takes in ever more of the true and the good. If people lived solely out of their own inclinations, likes and dislikes, the boundaries of their mind souls would coincide with those of their sentient souls.

This formation, in the midst of which the physical body can be seen as if in a cloud, can be called the human aura. When the essential nature of the human being is seen in the way that this book attempts to describe, it is supplemented and enriched by the measure of the aura.

• • •

In the course of our early development, a moment arrives when, for the first time in our lives, each of us experiences him- or herself as an independent being face to face with the rest of the world. For sensitive people, this is a significant experience. In his autobiography, the poet Jean Paul recounts this moment: [31]

Although I have never told anyone about it, I will never forget the experience of being present at the birth of my self-awareness. I can tell you the place and time exactly. One morning when I was a very small child, I was standing in the front door looking toward the woodpile on the left, when suddenly the inner vision, "I am an I," struck me like a lightning bolt from heaven. It has gone on shining ever since. My "I" had seen itself, for the first time and for all time. It is almost inconceivable that my memory could deceive me on this point, since no one else ever told me anything about it that I might have added to. It was an incident that took place veiled in my human holiest of holies, and its very

novelty gave permanence to the mundane circumstances surrounding it.[9]

We all know that little children refer to themselves, by
saying things like "Charlie's a good boy," or "Mary
wants that," and we find it appropriate that they should
speak about themselves as they would about someone
else, since they are not yet aware of their own independent existence. Consciousness of self has not yet been
born in them.[10] Through this consciousness of self, an individual achieves self-definition as an independent being,
separate from everything else, as "I."

By "I," a person means the total experience of his or her
being as body and soul. Body and soul are the vehicles of
the "I"; it works in them. Just as the physical body has its
center in the brain, the soul has its center in the "I." Our
sensations are stimulated from outside; our feelings assert
themselves as effects of the outer world; our will relates to

---

9. Jean Paul Friedrich Richter, 1763-1825. He first described this
experience in *Wahrheit aus Jean Pauls Leben. Kindheitsgeschichte
von ihm selbst geschrieben* (*The True Story of Jean Paul's Life: A
Childhood Autobiography*)[three books in two volumes], Breslau,
1826-1828, Book I, p. 53.

10. We have noted that little children refer to themselves in the third
person. What is important here is not how early children use the
word "I," but at what point they can connect the appropriate idea
with the word. Children may well hear the word from adults and then
use it without grasping the idea "I." In general, however, they start to
use the word relatively late, and this in itself points to an important
fact of development, namely that the *idea* "I" gradually unfolds out
of a vague *feeling* of "I."

the outer world by manifesting in outward-directed actions. Our "I," however, our actual individual essence, remains invisible. It is very telling that Jean Paul describes becoming aware of his "I" as "an incident. . .veiled in [the] human holiest of holies," because we are each totally alone with our own "I." This "I" is the self of each human being. We are justified in seeing the "I" as our true being, and may therefore describe body and soul as the "garments" in which we live, as the bodily conditions under which we act. In the course of our development we learn to use these instruments more and more as servants of our "I."

This little word "I," as it is used in our language, is a name different from all other names. Appropriate reflection on the nature of this name opens up an approach to understanding human nature in a deeper sense. Any other name can be applied to the corresponding object by all of us in the same way. Everyone can call a table "table" and a chair "chair." But this is not the case with the name "I." No one can use it to mean someone else; each of us can only call him- or herself "I." The name "I," if it designates *me*, can never reach my ear from outside. The soul can only designate itself as "I" from within, through itself. Thus, when we say "I" to ourselves, something begins to speak in us that has nothing to do with any of the worlds from which the above-mentioned "garments" are taken.

The "I" gains an ever-increasing mastery over body and soul, and this is expressed in a person's aura. The greater the mastery, the more differentiated, complex and richly colored the aura becomes. How the "I" affects the aura is visible to the seer, but the "I" itself is not; it is truly "veiled in [the] human holiest of holies."

The "I" takes in the rays of the light that shines as eternal light in each human being. Just as we gather up experiences of body and soul in the "I," we also allow thoughts of truth and goodness to flow into it. Sense-perceptible phenomena reveal themselves to our "I" from one side, the spirit from the other. Body and soul give themselves over to the "I" in order to serve it, but the "I" gives itself over to the spirit in order to be filled by it. The "I" lives within the body and the soul, but the spirit lives within the "I." What there is of spirit in the "I" is eternal, for the "I" receives its nature and significance from whatever it is united with. To the extent that it dwells in a physical body, it is subject to mineral laws; through the ether body it is subject to the laws governing reproduction and growth; by virtue of the sentient and mind souls it is subject to the laws of the soul world. And to the extent that it receives the spiritual into itself, it is subject to the laws of the spirit. What is formed in accordance with mineral laws and the laws of life comes into existence and passes away again; the spirit, however, has nothing to do with becoming and perishing.

• • •

[32]   The "I" dwells in the soul. Although the highest manifestation of the "I" belongs to the *consciousness soul*, it is also true that the "I" radiates outward from there, filling the entire soul and exerting its influence on the body

through the soul. And within the "I," the spirit is alive and active. The spirit streams into the "I," taking it as its "garment" just as the "I" itself lives in the body and the soul. The spirit shapes the "I" from the inside out and the mineral world shapes it from the outside in. We will call the spirit that shapes an "I," that lives as an "I," the spirit self, since it appears as the human "I" or "self."

We can explain the difference between the spirit self and the consciousness soul as follows: The consciousness soul merely touches the autonomous truth that is independent of all sympathy and antipathy, but the spirit self carries this same truth inside itself, taken up, enclosed and individualized by means of the "I" and taken into the individual's independent being. Through becoming independent and uniting with the truth, the "I" itself achieves immortality.

The spirit self is a revelation of the spiritual world within the "I," just as a sense perception, coming from the other side, is a revelation of the physical world within the "I." In what is red, green, light, dark, hard, soft, warm or cold, we recognize the revelations of the physical world; in what is true and good, the revelations of the spiritual world. Just as we call the revelation of physical things "sensation," we will call the revelation of spiritual things "intuition."[11] Even a very simple thought already contains intuition, because we cannot touch it with our hands

[33]

---

11. In my book *How to Know Higher Worlds* and in *Occult Science*, the real nature of intuition is described. Casual readers could easily imagine a discrepancy between how this term is used in those two books and its use here.

or see it with our eyes; we must receive its revelation from the spirit by means of the "I."

If a less developed and a more developed person look at the same plant, something quite different happens in the "I" of the first than in the "I" of the second, even though the sensations of both have been prompted by the same object. The difference is that one person can form much more complete thoughts about the object than the other. If objects revealed themselves only through sensation, there could be no progress in spiritual development. Members of primitive cultures also experience nature, of course, but natural laws become apparent only to the intuition-fructified thinking of the more highly developed person. Even children experience the stimuli of the outer world as incentives to their will, but the dictates of what is morally right become accessible to them only in the course of their development as they learn to live in the spirit and understand its revelations.

[34]   Just as there would be no sensations of color without the eye, there would also be no intuitions without the higher thinking of the spirit self. The sensation does not create the plant on which the color appears, nor does intuition create spiritual realities; it merely supplies information about them.

---

11. (continued) However, this contradiction does not exist if we observe closely and note that that element from the spiritual world that discloses itself in its full reality to spiritual perception by means of intuition announces itself in its *lowest* manifestation to the spirit self just as outer existence announces itself to the physical world by means of sensation.

Through intuitions, the "I," awakening in our soul, re-   *[35]*
ceives messages from above, from the spiritual world,
just as it receives messages from the physical world
through sensations. In this way, the "I" makes the spiritual world part of its personal soul life, just as it does with
the physical world by means of the senses. The soul, or
rather the "I" that is beginning to shine within it, opens its
doors on two sides, toward the physical world and toward
the spiritual.

The only way the physical world is able to make its pres-   *[36]*
ence known to our "I" is by building up, out of its own substances and forces, a body in which a conscious soul is
able to live and to take hold of the organs for perceiving
the external physical world. Similarly, the spiritual world,
with its spirit substances and spirit forces, builds up a spiritual body in which the "I" is able to live and to perceive
spiritual realities by means of intuitions. (Obviously, the
terms "spirit substance" and "spiritual body" are contra-
dictions in terms if taken literally. They are used here only
to direct our thoughts to the spiritual entity that corresponds to the physical human body.)

The physical body is built up within the physical world   *[37]*
as a completely separate being, and the same is true of the
spiritual body in the spiritual world. The human being
likewise has an inside and an outside in the physical
world, and the same is true in the spiritual world. And just
as we take in substances from our physical surroundings
and incorporate them into our bodies, we also take in spiritual substance from our spiritual surroundings and make
it our own. This spiritual substance is eternal nourishment

for human beings. We are born out of the physical world, and yet we are independent beings separate from the rest of the physical world. In the same way, we are born out of the spirit through the eternal laws of the good and the true, and yet we are separate from the spiritual world outside us. We will call this independent spiritual entity the "spirit body."[12]

[38]   When we examine a physical human body, we find the same substances and forces that are found outside it in the rest of the physical world. The same is true of the spirit body—the elements of the outer spiritual world pulsate in it; the forces of the rest of the spiritual world are active in it. In the physical world, a living and

---

12. Rudolf Steiner here uses the term *Geistesmensch*. Literally translated this means "spirit human being" or, as in previous translations, "Spirit Man." In theosophical language, and in the earliest editions of *Theosophy* itself, it is called Atman (as the spirit-self is called Manas and the Life-Spirit is called Budhi). It is clear from the present context, however, and from the conclusion—namely, that the *Geistesmensch* or "spirit human being" is the physical body transformed by the "I"—that "spirit body" is actually the most unambiguous and least confusing translation. Cf. *The Spiritual Hierarchies and their Reflection in the Physical World,* p. 44: "Outwardly the physical body appears a physical body, but inwardly it is completely controlled and permeated by the 'I'. At this stage, the physical body is both physical body and Atman." Also, *The Gospel of St. John*, p 36: "[The Human being] will finally reach the point where, by means of the 'I' he [or she] will transform the physical body also. That part of the physical body which is transformed by the 'I' is called Atman or Spirit Man." And p. 116: ". . .and the physical body will be so greatly metamorphosed that it will, at the same time, be as truly a Spirit Man, Atman, as it is now a physical body."

sentient being is closed off within a physical skin, and the same applies to the spiritual world. A membrane closes off the spirit body from the undifferentiated spiritual world and makes the spirit body a self-contained spiritual being within that world, a being that intuitively perceives the spiritual content of the universe. We will call this spiritual membrane the spiritual skin or "auric membrane." We must keep in mind, however, that this spiritual skin is constantly expanding to accommodate human development, and that the spiritual individuality of a human being (the auric membrane) is capable of unlimited expansion.

Inside the spiritual skin, the spirit body is alive; it is built up by a spiritual life force in the same sense that the physical body is built up by a physical life force. Therefore, just as we speak of an ether body, we must also speak of an ether spirit for the spirit body. We will call this ether spirit the life spirit. The spiritual constitution of the human being is thus subdivided into three members, the spirit body, the life spirit, and the spirit self. [39]

For someone who can "see" in spiritual regions, this spiritual constitution is a perceptible reality—the higher, truly spiritual portion of the aura. A seer can "see" the spirit body as life spirit inside the spiritual skin, can see how the life spirit constantly grows larger by taking in nourishment from the outer spiritual world, and can also see how, as a result, the spiritual skin continues to expand and the spirit body becomes larger and larger. Of course the spatial concept of "getting larger" is only an image of the actual reality. Nevertheless, in picturing this, we are [40] directed toward the corresponding spiritual reality. The difference between the human being as a spiritual being and as a physical being is that physical growth is restricted to a fixed size while spiritual growth can continue indefinitely. What is taken in as spiritual nourishment is of eternal value.

It follows that the human aura is made up of two interpenetrating parts, one of which is given form and color by our physical existence, the other by our spiritual existence. *[41]* The "I" provides the separation between the two: The physical relinquishes its distinctive character to build up a body that allows a soul to come to life, while on the other side the "I" does the same, allowing the spirit to have a life within it. The spirit in turn permeates the soul and gives it a goal in the spiritual world. Through the physical body, the soul is confined to physical existence; through the spirit body, it grows wings that give it mobility in the spiritual world.

• • •

[42] If we want to comprehend the human being as a whole, we must imagine that each individual is put together out of the components described above. The physical body builds itself up out of the world of physical substance in such a way that this structure meets the requirements of a thinking "I." This body is permeated by life force, thus becoming the ether body or life body. As such, it opens itself up to the outside in the sense organs, and becomes the soul body. The soul body is permeated by, and forms

a unity with, the sentient soul. The sentient soul not only receives the impressions of the outer world in the form of sensations but also has a life of its own that is fructified both by sensations from one side and by thinking from the other. Through this it can become the "mind soul." By being open to intuitions from above as well just as it is open to sensations from below, it becomes the consciousness soul. This is possible because the spiritual world builds the organ of intuition into it, just as the physical body builds the sense organs for it. The senses transmit sensations to it by means of the soul body; similarly, the spirit transmits intuitions to it by means of the organ of intuition. Thus the spirit body and the consciousness soul are linked in an entity analogous to the linking of the physical body and the sentient soul in the soul body. That is, the consciousness soul and the spirit self form a unity in which the spirit body lives as the life spirit, just as the ether body forms the living bodily basis for the soul body. And just as the physical body is contained within the physical skin, the spirit body is also contained within the spiritual skin. As a result, the entire human being is subdivided into the following members:

A. Material, physical body

B. Ether body or life body

C. Soul body

D. Sentient soul

E. Mind soul

F. Consciousness soul

G. Spirit self

H. Life spirit

I. Spirit body

[43]   The soul body (C) and sentient soul (D) are a unity in earthly human beings, as are the consciousness soul (F) and the spirit self (G). This yields seven components of the earthly human being:

1. The material, physical body

2. The ether or life body

3. The sentient soul body

4. The mind soul

5. The spirit-filled consciousness soul

6. The life spirit

7. The spirit body

[44]   Within the human soul, the "I" flashes up, receives the impact of the spirit and thus becomes the vehicle of the spirit body. Thus we each take part in three worlds—the physical, soul and spiritual worlds. We are rooted in the physical world through the material-physical body, ether body and soul body; we come to flower in the spiritual world through the spirit self, life spirit, and spirit body. But the stem, which roots at one end and flowers at the other, is the soul itself.

[45]   It is possible to give a simplified version of this subdivision of the human being that is in complete harmony

with the original. Although the human "I" lights up in the consciousness soul, it also permeates the entire being of the soul, whose members on the whole are less clearly separated than the components of the bodily organization and interpenetrate one another in a higher sense. If we look at the mind soul and the consciousness soul as the two garments of the "I" that belong together, with the "I" as their central core, then the human being can be differentiated into physical body, life body, astral body, and "I," with the term "astral body" designating the union of the soul body and the sentient soul. This term is common in older literature and is here freely applied to that aspect of the human being that lies beyond what is sense-perceptible. Although in a certain respect the sentient soul is also filled with forces by the "I," it is so intimately connected with the soul body that using a single term for the union of the two is justified.

When the "I" in turn imbues itself with the spirit self, this spirit self manifests in such a way that the astral body is worked over from within the soul. What is active in the astral body to begin with are our drives, desires and passions, to the extent that we perceive them, as well as our sense perceptions. Sense perceptions come about through the soul body, a member of our human constitution that comes to us from the outer world. Drives, desires, passions and so on originate in the sentient soul to the extent that it is filled with forces by our inner self before this inner self gives itself over to the spirit self. When the "I" imbues itself with the spirit self, the soul in turn fills the astral body with the spirit self's forces. As a result, drives, desires and passions are illuminated by what the "I" has received from the spirit. The "I" has then become master over the world of drives, desires and so on by virtue of its participation in the spiritual world. To the extent that this mastery takes place, the spirit self appears within the astral body, which is transformed as a result. The astral body then appears as a two-part entity, one part transformed and the other untransformed. For this reason, we may call the spirit self, in its manifestation in the human being, the transformed astral body.

A similar process takes place when we receive the life spirit into the "I." The life body is transformed by being imbued with the life spirit. That is, the life spirit manifests in such a way that the life body becomes something different. Thus we can also say that the life spirit is the transformed life body.

And again, if the "I" then takes the spirit body into itself, it receives the strong force, which it then uses to permeate the physical body. Of course, the part of the physical body that is thus transformed is not perceptible to the physical senses; this part that has been spiritualized has become the spirit body. The physical body as a physical thing is then perceptible to the physical senses, but to the extent to which it has been spiritualized, it must be perceived by spiritual faculties. To the outer senses, even the physical part that has been permeated by the spiritual appears to be purely physical.

Taking all of this as a basis, we can now present the following subdivision of the human being:

1. Physical body
2. Life body
3. Astral body
4. The "I" as the soul's central core
5. Spirit self as transformed astral body
6. Life spirit as transformed life body
7. Spirit body as transformed physical body

ADDENDUM

It may seem that the subdivisions of the human constitution presented in this book are based on purely arbitrary distinctions between parts within a monolithic soul life. To counter this objection, it must be emphasized that the significance of this phenomenon is similar to that of the appearance of the seven colors of the rainbow when light passes through a prism. What a physicist contributes to our understanding of light by studying this process and the seven colors that result is analogous to what the spiritual scientist does for our understanding of the makeup of the human soul. The soul's seven members are not abstract intellectual distinctions any more than are the light's seven colors. In both cases, the distinctions rest on the inner nature of the things themselves, the only difference being that the seven constituents of light become visible by means of an external device while the seven components of the soul become perceptible to a method of spiritual observation consistent with the nature of the human soul. The true nature of the soul cannot be grasped without knowing about this subdivision, because the soul belongs to the transitory world by virtue of three of our constitutional components—physical body, life body and soul body—and has its roots in eternity through the other four constituent parts.

When the soul is seen as a unity, its transitory and eternal aspects are indistinguishably bound up with each other, but unless we are aware of the differentiations within it, we cannot understand its relationship to the world as a whole. Let me use another comparison. Chemists separate water into hydrogen and oxygen, two substances that cannot be distinguished when they are united in the form of water. However, each of these elements has an identity of its own and can form compounds with other elements. Similarly, at death our three lower constitutional components unite with the makeup of the perishable world, while our four higher members unite with the eternal. Refusing to consider this differentiation within the soul is like being a chemist who refuses to learn about decomposing water into hydrogen and oxygen.

CHAPTER 2

DESTINY AND
THE REINCARNATION
OF THE SPIRIT

The soul lives and acts in the middle ground between [1]
body and spirit. The impressions reaching the soul
through the body are fleeting, present only as long as the
body's organs are open to the things of the outside world.
My eyes perceive the color of a rose only as long as they
are open and face to face with the rose. The presence of
both the outer-world object and the bodily organ is necessary in order for an impression, a sensation or a perception to come about.

However, what I recognize in my spirit as true about
the rose does not pass away with the present moment.
This truth is not at all dependent on me—it would be true
even if I had never experienced that rose. Whatever I
may recognize through the spirit is grounded in an element of the soul's life that connects the soul to a universal content, a content that reveals itself within the soul
but is independent of its transitory bodily basis. Whether
this content is imperishable in every respect does not

matter; what matters is that it be revealed in such a way that the soul's independent imperishable aspect, rather than its perishable bodily basis, is involved. The soul's enduring aspect comes into view as soon as we become aware of experiences that are not limited by its transitory aspect. Here, too, the important point is not whether these experiences first come to consciousness through transitory bodily processes, but whether they contain something that, although it lives in the soul, still possesses a truth independent of any transitory perceptual processes.

The soul stands between the present and the permanent in that it occupies the middle ground between body and spirit. However, it also mediates between the present and the permanent. It preserves the present for remembrance, wresting it away from perishability and giving it a place in the permanence of its own spiritual nature. The soul also puts the stamp of permanence on the temporal and temporary, since it does not simply give itself up to fleeting stimuli but also determines things out of its own initiative, incorporating its own essence into the actions it carries out. Through memory, the soul preserves yesterday; through action, it prepares tomorrow.

[2]   If my soul were not able to hold the red color of the rose through memory, it would have to perceive this red over and over again to be conscious of it. But whatever remains after the external impression is gone, whatever my soul can retain, can once again become a mental image or representation, independent of the external impression. Through this ability, my soul turns the outer world into its

own inner world by retaining the outer world through memory and continuing to lead an inner life with it, independent of any impressions acquired in the past. Thus the life of the soul becomes a lasting consequence of the transitory impressions made by the outer world.

But actions, too, acquire permanence once they have been stamped on the outer world. When I cut a branch from a tree, something that happens because of my soul totally changes the course of events in the outer world. Something quite different would have happened to that branch had I not intervened with my action. I have called up a series of consequences that would not have been present without me, and what I have done today will remain in effect tomorrow. It has become lasting through my action, just as yesterday's impressions have become lasting for my soul through memory. *[3]*

In our ordinary consciousness, we do not usually form a concept of "becoming lasting through action" in the same way that we form a concept of memory, of becoming lasting as a result of observation or perception. But is the "I" not just as strongly linked to a change in the world that results from its own action as it is to a memory that results from an impression? The "I" assesses new impressions differently, according to the memories it has or does not have, of one thing or of another. As an "I," however, it also enters into another relationship with the world that depends on whether it has carried out a certain action or another. Whether or not I made an impression on someone else through something I have done depends on the presence or absence of something in the relationship of *[4]* the world to my "I." I am a different person in my relationship to the world once I have made an impression on my environment. We do not notice this as easily as we notice how the "I" changes through acquiring a memory, but this is only because as soon as a memory is formed it unites with the overall life of the soul we have always regarded as our own, while the external consequence of an action, released from this soul life, goes on working through aftereffects that are quite different from what we can remember about the action. In spite of this, we must admit that something is now in the world as a result of our completed action, something whose character has been stamped on it by the "I."

Thinking this through carefully, we arrive at a question: Could it be that the results of our actions, whose character has been impressed on them by the "I," have a tendency to come back to the "I" in the same way that an impression preserved in memory comes to life again when an outer circumstance evokes it? What is preserved in memory is waiting for a reason to reappear. Could it be the same with things in the outer world that have been made lasting by the character of the "I"? Are they waiting to approach the soul from outside, just as a memory waits for a reason to approach from inside? This is only posed here as a question, since these results, laden with the character of our "I," may well never have any reason or opportunity to meet our soul again. However, if we follow this line of thought carefully, we can immediately see that such results could exist, and by their very existence determine the relationship of the world to the "I."

The next thing to investigate is whether anything in human life suggests that this conceptual possibility points to an actual reality.

. . .

Looking first at memory, we can ask how it comes [5] about. Obviously the process is quite different from how sensation or perception comes about. Without eyes, I could not have the sensation of blue. However, my eyes do not give me any memory of the blue; for them to provide the sensation, something blue must be in view at this moment. My bodily nature would allow all impressions to sink back down into oblivion if something were not also taking place in the relationship between the outer world and my soul—namely the formation of a current mental image through the act of perception, with the result that, through inner processes, I may later again have a mental image of something that originally brought about a mental image from *outside*. People who have become practiced at observing the soul will realize that it is all wrong to say that if I have a mental image today, the same mental image shows up again tomorrow in my memory, having stayed somewhere inside me in the meantime. On the contrary, the mental image that I have right now is a phenomenon that passes away with the present moment. But if memory intervenes, a process takes place in me that is the result of something additional that has gone on in the relationship between me and the outer world, something other than the evoking of the current mental image. The old mental image has not been "stored" anywhere; the one my memory calls up is a new one. Remembering means being able to visualize something anew; it does not mean that a mental image can come to life again. What appears today is something different from the original mental image. This point is being made because in the field of spiritual science it is necessary to form more precise concepts about certain things than we do in ordinary life, or even in ordinary science. Remembering means experiencing something that is no longer there, linking a past experience to my present life. This happens in every instance of remembering. Suppose I meet someone I recognize because I met him or her yesterday. This person would be a total stranger to me if I could not link the image formed through yesterday's perception to my impression of today. Today's image is given to me by perception, that is, by my sensory system. But who conjures up yesterday's image into my soul? It is the same being in me who was present at both yesterday's encounter and today's. Throughout the preceding discussion, this being has been called "the soul." Without this trusty keeper of the past, every external impression would be a new one for us. The soul imprints on the body the process by which something becomes a memory. However, the soul must first do the imprinting, and then perceive its imprint just as it perceives something outside itself. In this way, the soul is the keeper of memory.

[6]   As the keeper of the past, the soul is continually collecting treasures for the spirit. My ability to distinguish right from wrong is due to the fact that as a human being, I am

a thinking being capable of grasping truth in my spirit. The truth is eternal; even if I were continually losing sight of the past and each impression were new to me, the truth could still always reveal itself to me again in things. But the spirit in me is not restricted to the impressions of the moment; my soul widens the spirit's field of vision to include the past. And the more my soul can add to the spirit from the past, the richer the spirit becomes. The soul passes on to the spirit what it has received from the body. Thus, at every moment of its life, the human spirit carries two very different elements—first, the eternal laws of the true and the good; second, the recollection of past experiences. Whatever it does is accomplished under the influence of these two factors. Therefore, if we want to understand a human spirit, we must know two different things about it—first, how much of the eternal has been revealed to it, and second, how many treasures from the past it holds.

These treasures do not remain·in an unchanged form for [7] the spirit, however. The impressions we gain from experience gradually fade from memory, but their fruits do not. For example, we do not remember all the experiences we went through as children learning to read and write, but we would not be able to read or write now if we had not had these experiences and if their fruits had not been preserved in the form of abilities. This is how the spirit transforms its treasure trove of memories. It abandons to fate anything that can lead only to images of individual experiences, keeping only the power to heighten its own abilities. We can be sure that not a single experience goes to waste, since the soul preserves each one as a memory, and the spirit extracts from each one whatever it can use to enhance its abilities and enrich its life. The human spirit grows as these experiences are worked over and assimilated. Thus, although we do not find our past experiences preserved in the spirit as if in a treasure vault, we do find their effects in the abilities we have acquired.

· · ·

[8]   Until now, we have been considering the spirit and the soul only between birth and death, but we cannot leave it at that. That would be like considering the human body only within these same confines. Of course much can be discovered within them, but we will never be able to explain the human form through what exists between birth and death. This *Gestalt* cannot build itself up directly out of mere physical substances and forces; it must descend from another form or *Gestalt*, like itself, that has come about through reproduction. Physical substances and forces build up the body during its lifetime, while the forces of reproduction enable it to bring forth another body of the same form—that is, one that can be the carrier of the same life body. Every life body is a repetition of its immediate ancestor, and because this is so, the form the life body assumes is never arbitrary, but is the one that it has inherited. The forces that have made my human form possible came from my ancestors.

But the human spirit also assumes a definite form or *Gestalt* (the words are of course being used here in a spiritual sense). And human spiritual forms are as different as they can possibly be; no two individuals have the same spiritual form. Our observation in this realm must be as calm and objective as it is on the physical plane. We cannot maintain that the spiritual differences in people result only from differences in their environment, their upbringing and so on. That is not true at all, because two people from similar environments and of similar educational backgrounds can still develop in very different ways. We are forced to admit that they must have begun life with very different endowments.

At this point we are confronted with an important state of affairs which, if we recognize its full implications, sheds light on the essential nature and constitution of the human being. Of course if we choose to turn our attention only to the material aspect of events, we could say that the individual differences in human personalities result from genetic differences in the reproductive cells they develop from. If we take into account the laws of heredity discovered by Gregor Mendel and developed further by others, this point of view can indeed seem very plausible and also scientifically justifiable. Such a point of view, however, only demonstrates a lack of insight into how we really relate to our experience. Careful observation of the pertinent details will show that outer circumstances affect different people in different ways through something that never directly interacts with their material development. A precise researcher in this field will see that what proceeds from material potentials is separate and distinct from what may originate in our interaction with

our experiences but takes shape only because the soul itself enters into the interaction. Clearly, the soul relates to
something in the outer world that, through its very nature, has no connection to genetic potentials.

[9]   In our physical form or *Gestalt*, we are different from
the animals, our fellow creatures on the earth. Within certain limits, however, all human beings are of similar
form; there is only one human genus and species. No matter how great the differences between races, tribes, peo-
ples and personalities may be, in all physical respects the
similarity between two human beings is always greater
than that between a human being and an animal of any
species. Everything that comes to expression in the human species is determined by heredity, passed down from
one generation to the next. Our human form is bound to
this heredity. Just as a lion can inherit its physical form
only from its lion ancestors, we can inherit ours only from
our human ancestors.

[10]   The physical similarity between human beings is apparent to the eye, and the difference between human spiritual
forms is equally apparent to the unbiased spiritual view.
This is demonstrated by one very evident fact—that human beings have biographies. If we were nothing more
than members of our species, no individual biographies
would be possible. A lion or a pigeon is of interest only as
a member of the lion or pigeon species; we understand everything essential about the individual once we have described the species. It does not really matter whether we
are dealing with a parent, child or grandchild—what is interesting about them is common to all three generations.

What a human individual signifies, however, only begins where he or she stops being merely a member of a genus and species and becomes an individual being. I certainly cannot grasp the essential nature of Mr. John Doe by describing his son or his father—I have to know his own personal biography. If we think about the nature of biography, we will realize that with regard to the spirit, each human being is his or her individual genus.

Of course, if "biography" is interpreted to mean nothing more than a superficial listing of events and experiences, we might well insist that it would be possible to write the biography of a dog in the same sense as that of a person. However, if a biographer captures a human being's uniqueness, it will be clear that this biography of one human being corresponds to the description of an entire animal species. Obviously something resembling a biography can be written about an animal, especially an intelligent one, but that is not the point. The point is that a human biography corresponds to the description of an animal species rather than to the biography of an individual animal. Some people will always try to refute statements like this by saying that people who work with animals—zookeepers, for instance—are well aware of individual differences between animals of the same species. Such comments, however, demonstrate only an inability to distinguish individual differences from differences that can be acquired *only* through individuality.

Just as genus and species can be understood in a physical sense only once we grasp that they are determined by heredity, the individual spiritual being can be understood [11] only by means of a similar *spiritual heredity*. I possess my physical human form because I am descended from human ancestors. But where does what is expressed in my biography come from? As a physical human being, I repeat the form of my ancestors, but what do I repeat as a spiritual human being? If we insist that what my biography encompasses must simply be accepted as it is, that it needs no further explanation, we might as well also claim to have seen a hill out there where lumps of matter stuck themselves together into a living human being.

[12]   As a physical human being, I am descended from other physical human beings; I have the same form or *Gestalt* as the rest of the human genus. This shows that the characteristics of a genus are acquired within it through heredity. But as a spiritual human being, I have my own particular form, just as I have a personal biography. Therefore, I cannot have acquired this form from anyone other than myself. And since I came into this world, not with general, but with very specific predispositions of soul that have determined the course of my life as revealed by my biography, my work on myself cannot have begun at birth. I must have been present as a spiritual individual before my birth. I was certainly not present in my ancestors, because as spiritual individuals they are different from me, and their biographies cannot explain mine. Instead, I must—as a spiritual being—be the repetition of one whose biography can explain mine.

The only other conceivable possibility would be that I have only a spiritual life before birth (or conception) to thank for molding what my biography encompasses. This idea would be justifiable, however, only if we were to assume that what works on a human soul from its physical surroundings is of the same character as what the soul receives from a purely spiritual world. This assumption contradicts precise observation, however: What exerts a determining influence on a human soul from its physical surroundings works on it in the same way that a new experience works on a similar earlier experience in our physical life. To observe these relationships correctly, we must learn to perceive that some impressions in human life work on the soul's potentials in the same way that standing before something still to be done works on what we have already practiced repeatedly in physical life. Rather than affecting abilities acquired through practice in the course of this life, these impressions affect *potential* abilities of the soul. If we achieve insight into these things, we arrive at the idea of earthly lives that must have preceded this one. In thinking about it, we can no longer be content with assuming that this life is preceded only by purely spiritual experiences.

Schiller carried a physical form that he inherited from his ancestors; this physical form could not possibly have grown up out of the earth. The same is true of Schiller as a spiritual individuality; he must have been the repetition of another spiritual being whose biography accounts for his, just as human reproduction accounts for his physical form. The human physical form is a repetition or reembodiment, over and over again, of what is inherent in the human genus and species. Similarly, a spiritual individual must be a reembodiment or reincarnation of one and the same spiritual being, for as a spiritual being, each person is his or her own species.

[13]   We can object that what has been said here is a mere arrangement of thoughts, and we can demand external proof of it as we are accustomed to do in the case of ordinary science. However, it must be pointed out that the reincarnation of the spiritual human being is a process that does not belong to the domain of outer physical facts but takes place exclusively in the spiritual domain, and that of all our ordinary mental powers, only thinking has access to this realm. If we refuse to trust the power of thinking, we will never be able to explain higher spiritual facts to ourselves. But for anyone whose spiritual eye is open, the above train of thought is just as compelling as any process taking place in front of our physical eyes. Those who find a so-called "proof" constructed along the lines of ordinary scientific knowledge more persuasive than what has been presented about the significance of biography may well be great scientists in the usual sense of the word, but they are far removed from the methods of true spiritual research.

[14]   The attempt to explain a person's spiritual attributes as an inheritance from parents or other ancestors is evidence of a very dubious prejudice indeed. Those who are guilty of assuming that Goethe, for instance, inherited anything essential to his nature from his father and mother will probably not respond to reason, since they harbor a deep antipathy toward unbiased observation. Their materialistic persuasion prevents them from seeing relationships between phenomena in the right light.

What has been presented so far provides the prerequi- [15] sites for tracing our essential being beyond birth and death. Within the confines of birth and death, the human being belongs to the three worlds of bodily nature, soul nature and spirit nature. The soul forms the link between body and spirit by permeating the body's third member, the soul body, with the capacity for sensation and—as the consciousness soul—by pervading the first spiritual member, the spirit self. Throughout life, therefore, the soul participates in both body and spirit, and this partici- pation is expressed in all aspects of its existence. The or- ganization of the soul body determines to what extent the sentient soul can unfold its capacities; on the other hand, the consciousness soul's own life determines the extent to which the spirit self can develop within it. The better the soul body's development, the better the sentient soul can develop its interaction with the outer world; the more the consciousness soul supplies the spirit self with nourish- ment, the richer and more powerful the spirit self be- comes. During life, the spirit self is supplied with this nourishment through worked-over and assimilated expe- riences, and through their fruits, as has been demon- strated. Naturally, this interaction between soul and spirit can take place only where the two intermingle, that is, in the joining of the spirit self and the consciousness soul.

Let us look first at the interaction between the soul [16] body and the sentient soul. Although, as we have seen, the soul body is the most finely fashioned aspect of our bodily nature, it still belongs to and is dependent on this bodily nature. In one respect, the physical body, the ether body and the soul body form a totality. Therefore, the soul body is also subject to the laws of physical heredity through which the body receives its form, but since it is the most ephemeral aspect of our physical nature, it must also show the most ephemeral manifestations of heredity. Human physical bodies differ only slightly on the basis of race, nation and family, and although individual ether bodies vary more, they still show a great similarity. However, when it comes to the soul body, the differences are already very great. In the soul body, what we perceive as a person's external personal uniqueness is expressed; the soul body is therefore also the carrier of whatever personal uniqueness is passed down from ancestors to descendants.

It is true that the soul, as has been described, leads a full and independent life of its own—it shuts itself off with its likes and dislikes, emotions and passions. It is active as a totality, however, and the sentient soul, too, bears the stamp of this totality. Thus, because the sentient soul permeates and, so to speak, fills the soul body, the soul body takes shape in accordance with the nature of the soul and is then able, through heredity, to transmit the predecessor's inclinations, passions and so on to the descendants. Goethe's saying, "From my father, I get my build and the tendency to take life seriously; from my mother, my happy disposition and delight in storytelling,"[1] is based on this fact. But his genius, of course, did not come from

---

1. "*Vom Vater hab ich die Statur, des Lebens ernstes Führen; vom Mütterchen die Frohnatur, die Lust zu fabulieren.*"

either of his parents. This gives us an idea of what kinds of soul qualities are, in effect, turned over to the line of physical heredity.

The substances and forces of the physical body are present in the very same way all around us in outer physical nature—we are continually taking them in from outside and giving them back again. Over the course of a few years, all the substances that make up the physical body are renewed. They are continually being renewed, yet always take on the form of a human body because the ether body holds them together. And the ether body's form is not determined solely by processes taking place between birth (or conception) and death, but is also dependent on the laws of heredity that extend beyond birth and death. Because the soul body can be influenced by the sentient soul, characteristic soul qualities can also be transmitted through the line of heredity—that is, the soul has an impact on the process of physical heredity.

And what about the interaction between soul and spirit?   *[17]*
During life, the spirit is bound to the soul in the way described earlier. From the spirit, the soul receives the gift of living in the true and the good, and this enables it to bring the spirit itself to expression in its own life, in its inclinations, drives and passions. The spirit self brings the eternal laws of the true and the good to the "I" from the world of the spirit. By means of our consciousness soul, these laws are linked to the soul's own individual life experiences. These experiences are transitory, but their fruits are lasting; the fact that they have been linked to the spirit self makes a lasting impression on it. If the human

spirit then approaches such an experience and finds it similar to another that it has already been linked to in the past, it recognizes something familiar in it and knows that it must behave differently toward this than if it were encountering it for the first time. This is the basis of all learning. The fruits of learning are the abilities we acquire, and in this way, the fruits of our transitory life are imprinted on our immortal spirit.

Are we aware of these fruits in some way? Where do those potentials described above as characteristic of the spiritual human being come from? Surely they can only be based on the various capabilities people bring with them when they set out on their earthly journey. In some respects, these capabilities are quite like the ones we can acquire during our lifetime. Take the case of a genius, for instance. As a boy Mozart could write down from memory a long piece of music he had heard only once. He was able to do so only because he could survey the whole thing all at once, as a totality. In the course of our lifetime, we can all—at least within certain limits—broaden our capacity to gain an overview of things and to understand the relationships between them. We then possess new abilities. Lessing, for example, said that through his gift for critical observation, he had acquired something very close to genius. If we are not inclined to see such abilities, rooted in inborn potential, as miracles, we must see them as the fruits of what the spirit self has experienced through a soul. They have been impressed upon the spirit self, and since it did not happen in this lifetime, it must have happened in a previous one.

Each human spirit is a species in it own right. Just as individual human beings pass on their characteristics the spirit passes on its characteristics within its species—that is, within itself. *In each life the human spirit appears as a repetition of itself, with the fruits of its experiences in earlier lifetimes.* Thus this lifetime is the repetition of others, and brings with it what the spirit self has gained in its previous life. When the spirit self takes in something that can develop into fruit, it imbues itself with the life spirit. Just as the life body reproduces the form of a species from generation to generation, the life spirit reproduces the soul from one personal existence to the next.

The discussion up to this point has shown the validity   *[18]* of the idea that certain processes in human life can be explained in terms of repeated earth lives. The full significance of this idea can be realized only through the kind of observation that stems from spiritual insights such as those acquired by following the path to knowledge described at the end of this book. It should be pointed out that ordinary observation, properly guided by thinking, can lead us to this idea, although to begin with it will leave the idea in a shadow-like stage and will not be able to defend it completely against objections that arise from imprecise observation not properly guided by thinking. On the other hand, anyone who comes to this idea through ordinary thoughtful observation is preparing for supersensible observation by beginning to develop something we must have before supersensible observation can begin, just as we must have eyes before physical observation is possible. And people who object that by conceiving an idea like this we could talk ourselves into believing in the reality of supersensible perception, only prove themselves incapable of really taking up the truth through independent thinking; they are talking themselves into believing their own objections.

• • •

[19]   In this way the soul's experiences become lasting, not only within the confines of birth and death but also beyond death. But the soul imprints these experiences not only on the spirit lighting up within it, but also—by means of its actions—on the outer world, as has been pointed out. What someone did yesterday is still present today in the form of its effects.

Along these lines, the metaphor of sleep and death gives us a picture of the connection between cause and effect. Sleep has often been called "the younger brother of death." I get up in the morning. The continuity of my activity has been interrupted by the night. Under normal circumstances, I cannot resume my activity arbitrarily— I must link up with what I did yesterday if my life is to have any order and cohesiveness. Yesterday's actions are now the conditions I must abide by in what I do today; through what I did yesterday, I have created my destiny for today. I have disengaged myself from my own activity for a while, but it belongs to me and pulls me back again after I have withdrawn from it for a while. My past continues to be connected to me; it lives on in my present and will follow me into my future. Instead of waking up this morning, I would have to be created anew, out of nothing, if the effects of my actions from yesterday were not meant to be my destiny today. It would be as absurd as if under ordinary circumstances I had had a house built for myself and then did not move into it.

But we are not created anew each morning, nor is the [20] human spirit created anew as it starts the journey of its earthly life. We must try to understand what really does happen when we set out on this journey. A physical body makes its appearance, having received its form through the laws of heredity. This body becomes the vehicle for a spirit that is repeating an earlier life in a new form. Between the two, leading a self-contained life of its own, stands the soul. It is served by its likes and dislikes, and its wishes and desires, and places thinking in its service. As the sentient soul, it receives impressions from the outer world and carries them to the spirit, which extracts and preserves their fruits. The soul plays a mediator's role, in a sense, and its task is accomplished in playing this role satisfactorily. The body forms impressions for the soul, which reshapes them into sensations, stores them in the memory as mental images, and passes them on to the spirit to be made lasting. The soul is what actually makes us belong to this earthly life. Through the body, we belong to the physical human genus; we are members of this genus. With our spirit, we live in a higher world. The soul binds the two worlds together for a while.

On entering the physical world, the human spirit finds [21] itself, not in an unfamiliar setting, but in one that bears the imprint of its actions. Something in this new setting belongs to the spirit, bears the stamp of its being, is related to it. Just as the soul once conveyed impressions of the outer world to the spirit to be made lasting, it also, as the spirit's organ, transformed its spirit-given faculties into actions that, in their effects, are equally lasting. In doing so, the soul actually flowed into these actions. In the effects of its actions, the human soul lives on in a second independent life. This gives us grounds for examining how the processes of destiny enter into life. Something happens to us, "bumps into us," enters our life as if by chance—or so we tend to think at first. We can become aware, however, that each one of us is the result of many such "chance" occurrences. If at the age of forty I take a good look at myself and refuse to be content with an empty, abstract concept of the "I" as I ponder my soul's essential nature, I may well conclude that I am nothing more and nothing less than what I have become through what has happened to me until now as a matter of destiny. I would probably have been a different person if, at age twenty, I had had a different series of experiences than what actually did happen to me. I will then look for my "I" not only in its developmental influences that come from within, but also in what exerts a formative influence on my life from outside. I will recognize my own "I" in what "happens to" me.

If we give ourselves impartially to such a realization, we need to take only one more step in intimately observing life before we can see, in what comes to us through certain experiences of destiny, something that takes hold of the "I" from outside, just as memory works from inside to allow past experiences to light up again. In this way, we can become able to recognize an experience of destiny as a past action of the soul finding its way to the "I," just as a memory is a past experience that is reinvoked by outer circumstances and finds its way into our minds as a mental image.

The idea that the results of its own actions may meet the soul again has already been discussed as a possibility (See pp. 66ff). However, a meeting of this sort cannot come about within the confines of a single life on earth because this life has been organized and prepared in such a way as to bring about the action in question. The experience is intertwined with the accomplishment of the action. It is as impossible for a specific consequence of this action to return to the soul as it is for us to remember an experience when we are still in the middle of it. Rather, what comes into question here is our experience of consequences that meet the "I" when it does not have the aptitudes it had during the lifetime in which the action was performed— that is, it is only possible to focus on consequences that come from other earthly lives. As soon as we sense that some apparently coincidental experience is as closely related to the "I" as anything that takes shape out of the inner being of the "I," we can only conclude that in such an experience of destiny we are confronting consequences that come from earlier lives on earth. As we can see, an intimate, thought-guided approach to life leads us to adopt the idea (paradoxical as it may seem to our ordinary consciousness) that what we experience as destiny in one lifetime is related to our actions in previous earthly lives.

Once again, the full import of this idea can be realized only through supersensible knowledge, without which it remains shadow-like at best. But here too, the idea acquired by means of ordinary consciousness prepares our soul for witnessing its full truth through genuine supersensible perception.

[22]   However, only one part of my action is out in the world; the other part is in me. We can take a simple parallel from the field of biology to clarify the relationship between an "I" and its actions. In certain caves in Kentucky are animals that were able to see when they first ventured in, but have lost their sight through prolonged living in darkness. Their eyes have stopped functioning; the physical and chemical activity taking place during seeing no longer happens in them, and the stream of nutrients that once supported this activity has been redirected to other organs. By now, these animals can live only in caves. Through their original action, migrating into the caves, they have determined the conditions under which they must now live. Their migration has become a part of their destiny or fate. A being that was active in the past has linked itself to the results of its own actions. It is the same with the human spirit. Only by being active could the soul transmit certain capabilities to the spirit; these capabilities correspond directly to actions. An action that the soul has carried out gives it the strength and potential to carry out another action which is the direct fruit of the first. The soul carries this around as an inner necessity until the second action has been completed. We could also say that through an action, the

need to carry out its consequence is impressed on the soul.

Through its actions, each human spirit has truly pre- [23] pared its own destiny. It finds itself linked in each new lifetime to what it did in the previous one. We may wonder how that could possibly be, since the reincarnating spirit finds itself in a world totally different from the one it left behind. The way we conceive of the chain of destiny when we ask such a question, however, clings to quite external and superficial aspects of life. If my field of activity is shifted from Europe to America, I will also find myself in totally new surroundings, and yet my life in America will still be quite dependent on how I used to live in Europe. If I was a mechanic in Europe, my life in America will take shape quite differently than it would if I was a banker. In the first instance, I will probably be surrounded by machinery again in America; in the second, by the trappings of the banking business. In each case, my former life determines my surroundings; it extracts from the entire surrounding world those things that are related to it, so to speak. It is the same with the spirit self. In a new life, it is obliged to surround itself with things it is related to from its previous life.

That is why sleep is a helpful image for death, because during sleep we are also withdrawn from the arena in which our destiny awaits for us. While we are sleeping, events in this arena continue without us, and for a while we have no influence on the course they take. Nevertheless, how we live the next day still depends on the effects of what we did the day before. In reality, our personalities are reembodied anew each morning in the world of our actions. It is as if what we were separated from during the night is spread out around us during the day. The same holds true for the actions we carried out in earlier incarnations. They are bound to us as our destiny, just as dwelling in dark caves is bound to the animals who lost their sense of sight through migrating into those caves. Just as these animals can live only in the surroundings in which they now find themselves, surroundings into which they have inserted themselves, a human spirit *can* live only in the environment it has created for itself through its own actions. The ongoing course of events sees to it that when I wake in the morning, I find myself in a situation that I myself created the previous day. Similarly, my reincarnating spirit's relationship to the objects in the surroundings sees to it that I enter an environment corresponding to my actions in the previous life.

From the above, we can form an idea of how the soul is incorporated into the overall organization of a human being. The physical body is subject to the laws of heredity. The human spirit, on the other hand, must reincarnate over and over again, and its law consists in having to carry the fruits of previous lifetimes over into the following ones. Our souls live in the present, although this life in the present is not independent of our previous lives, since each incarnating spirit brings its destiny along with it from previous incarnations, and this destiny determines its present life. What impressions our souls will be capable of receiving, which of our desires can be fulfilled, what joys and sorrows will be our lot, what other human beings we will meet—all this depends on what our actions were like in earlier incarnations of the spirit. People to whom our souls were connected in one lifetime will necessarily encounter us again in a later one, because the actions that took place between us must have their consequences. Souls that have once been associated will venture into reincarnation at the same time. Thus, the life of the soul is a product of the spirit's self-created destiny.

The course of a human life within the framework of life and death is determined in three different ways, and we are also therefore dependent on three factors that go beyond birth and death. The body is subject to the laws of *heredity*; the soul is subject to self-created destiny or, to use an ancient term, to its *karma*; and the spirit is subject to the laws of *reincarnation* or repeated earthly lives. The interrelationship of body, soul and spirit can also be expressed as follows: The spirit is immortal; birth and death govern our bodily existence in accordance with the laws of the physical world; and the life of the soul, which is subject to destiny, mediates between body and spirit during the course of an earthly life. These three worlds to which we belong will be the subject of the next section of this book, since some familiarity with them is a prerequisite for all further knowledge of the essential nature of the human being.

If our way of thinking comes to grips with life's phe- *[24]* nomena and does not hesitate to follow thoughts resulting from living, vital observation through to their final ramifications, we can indeed arrive at the idea of repeated earthly lives and the law of destiny through mere logic. It is true that for a seer with opened spiritual eyes, past lives are present as a direct experience, like reading from an open book, but it is equally true that the truth of all of this can come to light for anyone with an active, observant reasoning ability.

ADDENDUM

The statements in this chapter on reincarnation and karma attempt to convey the extent to which human life and destiny point in and of themselves to the idea of repeated earth lives. The intent was to do so by thoughtfully considering the course of human life without referring to the spiritual scientific ideas presented in other chapters. Of course the very idea of reincarnation and karma will seem rather questionable to anyone who accepts only ideas that assume the existence of only a single earthly life as being well founded. However, the intention of this chapter is to show that such ideas cannot lead to an understanding of why a person's life takes a particular course. In that case we are forced to look for different ideas, which may appear to contradict our usual ones. The only reason for not looking for them would be a fundamental refusal on our part to apply the same thoughtful consideration with which we investigate physical processes to processes that can be grasped only inwardly. This refusal would mean, for instance, that we belittle the fact that our experience of a stroke of destiny bears a resemblance to what we experience when our memory encounters an event related to something we actually recollect. But if we try to see how a stroke of destiny is really experienced, we can distinguish between the real state of affairs and what can be said about such an experience from a merely external point of view that denies any vital connection between this stroke of destiny and our "I." From this point of view, a stroke of destiny appears to be either a coincidence or something determined from outside. And since in fact some strokes of destiny actually are making their first impact on a human life, so to speak, and only show their results later on, the temptation is all the greater to generalize from such instances without taking any other possibility into account.

We begin to consider other possibilities only once life has educated our cognitive abilities and brought them into line with what Goethe's friend Knebel once wrote in a letter:

> On close observation, we will find that most people's lives contain a plan that seems laid out for them either in their own character or in the circumstances that guide them. No matter how changeable and varied their situations may be, in the end a certain wholeness or inner coherence is apparent.... The hand of a specific fate, no matter how hidden its working, is still clearly to be seen, whether moved by outer causes or by inner impulses. Often, in fact, we are moved in its direction for quite conflicting reasons. No matter how confused the course of a life may be, a plan and a direction still show through.*

Raising objections to an observation of this sort is easy, especially for people unwilling to consider the inner experiences it stems from. However, the author of this book believes that in what he has said about destiny and repeated earth lives, he has accurately delineated the boundaries within which it is possible to form conceptions about the causes shaping human life. He has pointed out that the conviction to which these thoughts lead is only sketchily defined by them, that all they can do is prepare us in thought for what must ultimately be discovered by means of spiritual research. In itself, however, as long as this thought preparation does not exaggerate its own importance or attempt to prove anything, but only trains our soul, it entails an inner effort that can make us unbiased and receptive to facts we would simply take for foolish without it.

*Karl Ludwig von Knebel, 1744-1834. This letter appears in *K. L. v. Knebels literarischer Nachlass und Briefwechsel* ("K. L. von Knebel's Literary Legacy and Correspondence"), ed. K. A. Varnhagen von Ense & T. Mundt, 2nd ed., 1840, vol. 3, p. 452.

CHAPTER 3

THE
THREE WORLDS

I. The Soul World

We have seen that as human beings we belong to three [1] worlds. The substances and forces that build up our bodies are taken from the world of inanimate matter. We know about this world through the perceptions of our outer physical senses. Anyone who trusts these senses exclusively and develops only their kind of perception cannot gain access to the other two worlds, the soul and spiritual worlds. Whether or not we can persuade ourselves of the reality of any being or thing depends on our having an organ of perception, a sense, for it. Of course misunderstandings can easily arise when the higher organs of perception are referred to as spiritual "senses," as they are here. When we speak about "senses," we automatically think of something physical. We even call the physical world the "sense world" in contrast to the "spiritual world." In order to avoid misunderstanding, it must be emphasized that the term "higher senses" is used here only figuratively and as a comparison. Just as our physical senses perceive what is physical, our soul and spiritual senses perceive what is of a soul and spiritual nature. The term "sense" will be used here only in its meaning of "organ of perception."

Without eyes that are sensitive to light, we would have no knowledge of light or of color, just as we would have no knowledge of sound without ears that are sensitive to it. In this connection, the German philosopher Lotze is perfectly justified in saying:

> Without a light-sensing eye and a sound-sensing ear, the whole world would be dark and silent. It would be as impossible to have light and sound in it as it is to have a toothache without the pain-sensing nerve.[1]

To see all of this in the right light, we need only to imagine how different the world that we human beings know must appear to lower forms of animal life that possess only a sense of touch of a sort, spread out over the surface of their bodies. Light, color and sound cannot possibly be present for them in the sense that they are for beings endowed with eyes and ears. The vibrations in the air set off by firing a gun, for example, may also have some effect on these animals if they are actually touched by them, but for these vibrations to register in the soul as a shot, an ear is necessary, just as an eye is necessary if

---

1. Rudolf Hermann Lotze, 1817-1881, physician and philosopher active in Leipzig, Göttingen and Berlin. *Grundzüge der Psychologie* ("Fundamentals of Psychology"), Leipzig, 1894, p. 19.

certain processes taking place in the very fine matter we know as ether are to appear as light and color.

We can know something about the nature of a being or thing only because it has an effect on one of our organs. This relationship between the human being and the world of realities is admirably expressed by Goethe:

> In reality, any attempt to express the inner nature of a thing is fruitless. What we perceive are effects, and a complete record of these effects ought to encompass this inner nature. We labor in vain to describe a person's character, but when we draw together his actions, his deeds, a picture of his character will emerge.
>
> Colors are the deeds of light, what it does and what it endures.... Although it is true that colors and light are intimately related to one another we must consider both as belonging to all narure. Through them nature in its entirety seeks to manifest itself, in this case to the sense of sight, to the eye.
>
> Similarly, the whole of nature reveals itself to yet another sense.... [It] speaks *to other senses* which lie even deeper, to known, *misunderstood, and unknown senses.* Thus it converses with itself and with us through a thousand phemomena, *No one who is observant will ever find nature dead or silent.*[2] (Italics added)

---

2. *Scientific Studies: Goethe*, ed. and trans. Douglas Miller (New York: Suhrkamp Publishers, 1988), p.158.

Goethe's statement should not be interpreted as denying the possibility of understanding the essential nature of things. He does not mean that we perceive only the effects of things while their true nature remains concealed behind these effects; rather, he means that we should not talk about a "concealed nature" at all. The being is not *behind* its manifestation, but comes into view through its manifestation. However, this being may be so rich that it can disclose itself in other forms when appearing to other senses. What is disclosed does belong to the being in question, but because of the limitations of our senses, it is not the *whole* being. Goethe's view of this is the same as the spiritual scientific one presented here.

[2]   Within our body, our eyes and ears develop as organs of perception, as senses for bodily processes. Similarly, we can develop soul and spiritual organs of perception that will open up soul and spirit worlds to us. For anyone who does not have such higher senses, these worlds are dark and silent, just as the physical world is dark and silent to a being without eyes and ears. However, we relate differently to these higher senses than to our physical ones, which as a rule are fully developed in us by good Mother Nature without our doing anything about it. But we ourselves must work at developing our higher senses. Just as nature develops our physical body so that we can

2. (continued) See also Volume III of *Goethes Naturwissenschaftliche Schriften* (*Goethe's Scientific Works*), edited and with commentary by Rudolf Steiner, in Kürschner's *Deutsche National-Literature* (*Literature of the German Nation*) in five volumes, 1884-97. Reprinted in Dornach, 1975, GA 1a-e.

perceive our physical surroundings and orient ourselves in them, so we must cultivate our own soul and spirit if we want to perceive the soul and spirit worlds.

There is nothing unnatural about cultivating the higher organs that nature itself has not yet developed, because in a higher sense, everything that human beings accomplish also belongs to nature. Only those who contend that we should all stay at the level of development where nature left us could call developing these higher senses "unnatural." For such people, these organs and their significance are "mis-known" in Goethe's sense. Such people might as well oppose any and every kind of education for human beings—because that too goes beyond the work of nature—and should also be especially opposed to operating on anyone who was born blind. What happens to a blind person after a successful operation is very much like what happens to those who awaken their higher senses in the way described in the last section of this book. The world now appears to them full of new qualities, new processes and new facts that their physical senses never revealed. They see clearly that there is nothing arbitrary or capricious about supplementing reality through these higher organs, and that without these organs the essential part of this reality would have remained hidden from them. The soul and spirit worlds are not "next to" or "outside" the physical world, not separated from it in space. The formerly dark world is suddenly radiant with light and color for a person born blind who has undergone an operation. Similarly, the soul and spiritual qualities of things that until now had appeared to us only in a purely physical way are revealed when we are awakened in soul and spirit. Of course this new world is also full of occurrences and beings that remain totally unknown to anyone who has not undergone a soul and spiritual awakening. (Later on in this book, the development of the soul and spiritual senses will be discussed in greater detail, but first the higher worlds themselves will be described. Those who deny the existence of these worlds only demonstrate that they have not yet developed their own higher organs. Human development is never complete at any given level; it must always be taken further.)

[3]   We often tend, unintentionally, to imagine these higher organs as being too much like our physical ones. It is important to remember that these organs are soul or spiritual formations and that we must not expect what we perceive in the higher worlds to be only a misty and diluted form of material substance. As long as we expect anything of that sort, we will not come to a clear idea of what is actually meant here by "higher worlds." Many people would find it much easier to actually know something—at first, of course, only the elementary facts—about these higher worlds if they did not imagine that what they are to perceive is a highly refined version of something physical. That they make this assumption usually means that they do not want to recognize what is really involved. They find it unreal, do not accept it as something that could satisfy them, and so on. True, the higher levels of spiritual development are difficult to reach, but the levels adequate for recognizing the nature of the spiritual world—and that is already a lot—would

not be nearly as difficult to reach if people would first get rid of the prejudice that makes them imagine that what is of a soul and spiritual nature is simply a more refined version of what is physical.

We obviously do not really know a person if we have only an idea of his or her physical appearance, nor do we really know the world around us if we know only what our physical senses can tell us about it. A photograph becomes intelligible and full of life to us once we come to know the person in the photograph so well that we know his or her soul, and in the same way, we can really understand the material world only once we know its soul and spiritual basis. That is why it is good to talk first about the higher worlds of soul and spirit, and only then come to conclusions about the physical world from a spiritual scientific point of view. *[4]*

Certain difficulties are involved in talking about higher worlds at the present stage of civilization. The greatness of our age is due above all to its knowledge and mastery of the physical world. Our very words bear the stamp and meaning of the physical world, and yet using these ordinary words is our only possible link to what is familiar. This leaves the door wide open for misunderstanding by those willing to trust only their outer senses, since at first much can be expressed or indicated only through comparison and imagery. This, however, is how it has to be, because such images are a means of directing ourselves toward these higher worlds and fostering our eventual access to them. (We will speak about the ascent to higher worlds in a later chapter in which the development of the *[5]*

soul and spiritual organs of perception will be discussed.[3]
Indeed, to begin with, becoming aware of higher worlds
by means of comparisons is exactly what we *should* be doing. Only then can we contemplate learning to see them for
ourselves.)

[6]   Just as the substances and forces that constitute and govern our stomach, heart, lungs, brain and other organs come
from the material world, our soul qualities—our urges, desires, feelings, passions, wishes, sensations and so on—
come from the soul world. The human soul is a member of
this soul world just as the body is a part of the physical
world. If we want to cite a preliminary difference between
the physical and soul worlds, we can say that the latter is
much finer, more mobile and more malleable than the
former. Meanwhile, of course, we have to realize that we
are entering a totally new world when we come to the soul
world, and that when we call things "coarser" or "finer" in
this context, we are drawing comparisons between things
that are actually fundamentally different. The same applies to everything we can say about the soul world using
words borrowed from the physical. Taking this into consideration, we can say that the formations and beings of
the soul world consist of soul substances and are guided by
soul forces just as is the case with physical substances and
forces in the physical world.

---

3. These spiritual organs of perception, also discussed briefly in a
later chapter entitled "The Path to Knowledge," are dealt with in
greater detail in my books *How to Know Higher Worlds* and *Occult
Science*.

Just as occupation of space and movement within space   [7]
are characteristic of physical forms, so are impelling desires and responsiveness to stimuli characteristic of the
things and beings of the soul world. Thus we can also call
the soul world the world of desires, wishes or longing.
These expressions are all borrowed from the world of the
human soul, so we must keep in mind that in parts of the
soul world lying outside the human soul, things are as different from the soul forces within the human soul as the
substances and forces of the outer physical world are
from those that constitute the physical human body.
("Urge," "wish" and "longing" are terms describing the
soul world's "material," which we will call "astral substance." If we pay more attention to the soul world's
forces, we can use the term "desire being," but we must
not forget that the distinction here between matter and
force or energy cannot be as strict as it is in the physical
world. An urge can just as well be called a "force" as a
"substance.")

These differences between the soul and physical worlds   [8]
can be bewildering for anyone looking into the soul world
for the first time, but the same is true when a previously
inactive physical sense opens and starts to function. After
eye operations, people who were born blind must also
learn to orient themselves in a world they used to know
only through the sense of touch. At first, they see the objects as if these were actually in their eyes; next they see
them outside their eyes, but as if painted on a flat surface.
Only gradually do they learn to perceive depth and the
spatial distance between things.

The laws in effect in the soul world are entirely different from the ones in effect in the physical world, although of course many soul formations are linked to
those of the other worlds. The human soul, for example,
is linked to the human physical body and to the human
spirit, and the processes observable in it are influenced
by both the physical and spiritual worlds. We must take
this into account when observing the soul world, and we
must not make the mistake of attributing to a law of the
soul world what is actually due to the influence of one of
the other worlds. For example, when a wish proceeds
from a human being, it is carried by a thought, a spiritual
conception, whose laws it obeys. But just as we can establish what the laws of the physical world are by disre-
garding the influence human beings have on its
processes, for example, we can do something similar
with the soul world.

[9]   We can express an important difference between soul
and physical processes by saying that the interaction between soul processes is much more inward. In physical
space, for instance, the law of impact is in effect. If a
moving ivory ball strikes another one at rest, the second
ball moves in a direction that can be calculated from the
motion and elasticity of the first. In soul space, however,
the interaction between two formations that meet depends
on their inner attributes. If they are related, they interpenetrate and grow together, so to speak. If their essential natures are in conflict, they repel each other. To take
another example, certain laws govern the way we see
things in physical space—distant objects appear reduced

in size. When we look down a long tree-lined street, the trees in the distance, in accordance with the laws of perspective, appear closer together than the ones in the foreground. But in soul space all things, near and far, appear to the observer at distances from one another that are determined by their inner nature. Of course this can be a source of any number of errors for anyone who enters soul space and tries to get along using rules brought from the physical world.

One of the first things we must learn in order to orient   *[10]*
ourselves in the soul world is to distinguish the different types of formations, just as we distinguish between solid, liquid and gaseous bodies in the physical world. To do this, we need to be aware of the two basic forces that are all-important here, which may be called *sympathy* and *antipathy*. How these fundamental forces work within a soul formation determines its type. *Sympathy* is the force with which soul formations attract each other, try to merge with each other, and let their affinity take effect. *Antipathy*, on the other hand, is the force through which soul formations repel and exclude each other, and maintain their own identity. The role a soul formation plays in the soul world depends on the extent to which these basic forces are present in it. First we must distinguish three types of soul formations on the basis of how sympathy and antipathy act in them. These types differ in their specific inner interrelationships of sympathy and antipathy, but *both* basic forces are present in all three.

When we look at a soul formation of the first type, we find that it attracts other formations in its surroundings by means of the sympathy at work within it. But in addition to this sympathy, antipathy is also present at the same time, causing the formation to repel certain things in its surroundings. Seen from outside, this type of formation appears to possess only antipathetic forces, but that is not the case. Both sympathy and antipathy are present in it, but the latter is dominant. Formations like this play a self-centered role in soul space, repelling much of what surrounds them and lovingly attracting relatively little. Thus, they move through soul space as unchangeable forms. The force of sympathy present in them makes them appear greedy, and their greed appears insatiable, as though it could never be satisfied, since their prevailing antipathy repels so much of what approaches them that no satisfaction can occur. If we were to compare soul formations of this type to something in the physical world, we might say that they correspond to solid physical bodies. This region of soul substance can be called "burning desire." The portion of this burning desire that is included in animal and human souls determines what we know as their lower sensual urges, their prevailing self-serving instincts.

In the second type of soul formation, the two basic forces are held in balance; that is, sympathy and antipathy work equally strongly. Formations of this sort approach others with a certain neutrality, acting as if they were related but without especially attracting or repelling them. They do not draw any fixed boundaries between themselves and their surroundings, so to speak, and constantly allow themselves to be influenced by other formations around them. For these reasons, they can be compared to fluid substances in the physical world. There is no trace of greed in the way such formations draw others toward them. The kind of activity meant here is evident, for instance, when the soul receives a sensation of color. If I have the sensation of a red color, I am receiving a stimulus from my surroundings, a stimulus that is *neutral* to begin with. Only when my liking for red is added to the stimulus does another soul activity enter the picture. The neutral stimulus is caused by soul formations in which a balanced interaction between sympathy and antipathy is maintained. We must describe the soul substance in question as totally malleable and flowing. When it moves through soul space, it is not self-centered like the first type; its existence is constantly receptive to impressions, and it shows a relationship to much of what comes to meet it. "Flowing sensitivity" is a term that might be applied to this second type.

In the third type of soul formations, sympathy predominates over antipathy. Antipathy brings about self-centered self-assertion; in this case, however, it takes second place to inclination toward things in the surroundings. We can imagine a formation like this in soul space. It appears as the center of a sphere of attraction reaching out over the objects in its surroundings. An appropriate term for these particular formations is "wish substantiality." This seems to be the right designation because the effect of the antipathy present in them, although it is weaker than the sympathy, is to bring the objects the formation attracts into its own sphere of influence, thus giving the sympathy in it a fundamental note of self-seeking. This wish substantiality can be compared to airy or gaseous bodies in the physical world, since it spreads out in all directions, just as a gas naturally tries to expand on all sides.

[11]   The higher levels of soul substance are characterized by the total withdrawal of one of the fundamental forces, namely antipathy; only sympathy exhibits any effectiveness. It can now begin to assert itself within the parts of the soul formation so that these parts attract each other. The force of sympathy within a soul body comes to expression in what we call *pleasure*; any reduction in sympathy is called *displeasure*. Displeasure is simply diminished pleasure, just as cold is diminished heat. Pleasure and displeasure constitute what lives in the world of *feelings*—in the narrower sense—within a human being. *Feeling* is the soul's weaving activity within itself, and what we call our "comfort" depends on how feelings of pleasure and displeasure mingle in our soul.

[12]   A still higher level is occupied by the soul formations whose sympathy is not confined to the domain of their own lives. They, as well as the above-mentioned fourth level, differ from the three lower levels in that the force of sympathy no longer has any counteractive antipathy to overcome. Only through these higher forms of soul substance can the many different soul formations unite into a common soul world. As long as any antipathy is involved, a soul formation strives toward other things for the sake of its own life, in order to strengthen and enrich itself through the other. When antipathy is silent, the other is received as revelation, as information. In soul

space, this higher form of soul substance plays a role similar to that of light in physical space. It causes one soul formation to absorb the being and essence of others for their own sake, or, as we might also put it, lets itself be shone upon by them. Soul beings first awaken to true soul life by drawing from these higher regions. Their subdued life in the darkness opens up to the outside and starts to shine and radiate out into soul space; their dull and sluggish inner movement, which attempts to shut itself off by means of antipathy when only the substances of the lower regions are present, is transformed into power and mobility pouring out from within. The flowing sensitivity of the second region comes into effect only on contact, when soul formations meet, in which case one flows over into the other. Actual contact is necessary here. But in the upper regions a free outraying and outpouring is the rule. (It is quite justified to characterize the essence of this region as "raying out," since the sympathy developed here works in such a way that this expression derived from the working of light can surely be used as its symbol.) A soul formation without the enlivening soul substances of the higher regions grows stunted like a plant in a dark cellar. *Soul light, active soul power* and *soul life* itself—in the narrower sense—belong to these regions and from here impart themselves to the soul beings.

We must thus distinguish three lower and three upper [13] regions of the soul world and a fourth that mediates between them, yielding the following subdivision of the soul world:

1. Region of burning desire
2. Region of flowing sensitivity
3. Region of wishes
4. Region of pleasure and displeasure
5. Region of soul light
6. Region of active soul power
7. Region of soul life

[14]   In the first three regions, soul formations receive their characteristic qualities from the inner relationship between antipathy and sympathy; in the fourth, sympathy moves and works within a soul formation itself; in the three highest regions, the force of sympathy becomes ever freer. The soul substances of these highest regions waft through soul space, enlightening and enlivening, awakening what would, if left to itself, lose itself in its own existence.

[15]   Although it should be unnecessary to mention it by now, let us emphasize for the sake of clarity that these seven divisions of the soul world do not represent distinct and separate areas. Just as solid, fluid and gaseous substances intermingle in the physical world, burning desires, flowing sensitivity and the forces of the world of wishes interpenetrate in the soul world. On the physical level, heat penetrates and light shines on bodies; in the soul world, the same thing happens with pleasure and displeasure, and with soul light. Something similar is also true of active soul power and soul life.

II. The Soul in the Soul World after Death

The human soul is the connecting link between the human spirit and the human body. Its forces of sympathy and antipathy—which through their interplay bring about the soul's expressions of desire, sensitivity, wish, pleasure and displeasure, and so on—are not only active between soul formations, but also express themselves in relationship to the beings of the other worlds, the physical and the spiritual. While the soul is living in a body, it participates to some degree in everything that goes on in this body. When the functions of the physical body are proceeding smoothly, pleasure and comfort arise in the soul, but when these functions are disturbed, displeasure and pain appear. But the soul also takes part in the spirit's activities—one thought fills it with joy, another with disgust; it applauds a correct judgment and disapproves of a false one. A person's level of development depends on whether his or her soul leans more in the one direction or in another. Individuals are the more nearly perfect the more their souls sympathize with manifestations of the spirit, the less perfect the more their souls' inclinations are satisfied through bodily functions. [16]

The spirit is at the center of each human being, and the body is the instrument through which the spirit observes and knows, and also acts in, the physical world. The soul, however, mediates between the two. For example, it releases the sensation of tone from the physical impressions that air vibrations make on the ear, and then it experiences pleasure in this tone. It imparts all this to the spirit, which [17] grows in its understanding of the physical world as a result. A thought that appears in the spirit is converted by the soul into the wish to bring the thought into being, and only then—with the help of the bodily instrument—can the thought become an accomplished *deed*. We human beings can live up to our calling only by letting all of our activity be directed by the spirit. Left to itself, the soul can as easily turn its inclinations toward the physical world as toward the spiritual; its "feelers," so to speak, extend down into the physical as well as up into the spirit. Through this extension into the physical world below, the soul's own essential being is permeated and colored by the nature of this physical world. And since the spirit can only work in the physical world by means of the soul's mediation, the spirit itself points in the direction of the physical. Its formations are drawn toward the physical through the forces of the soul.

Consider undeveloped human beings. Their souls' inclinations are closely linked to their bodily functions. They experience pleasure only through the impressions the physical world makes on their senses. Even their mental activity is completely drawn down into this sphere; their thoughts serve only to satisfy the needs of their physical existence. But as the spiritual self proceeds from incarnation to incarnation, its orientation is meant to be provided increasingly by the spirit, its knowledge determined by the spirit of eternal truth and its activity by eternal goodness.

[18]   Death is a fact of the physical world that signifies a change in the functioning of the body. At death the body

ceases to be a vehicle for a soul and a spirit, and from then on its functions become totally subject to the physical world and physical laws. It passes into the physical world in order to disintegrate in it. Our physical senses can observe only what happens to the body after death; what happens to the soul and spirit eludes them. Even when a person is alive, the soul and spirit can be observed only to the extent that they take on an outer manifestation in physical processes. After death, this is no longer possible. Therefore, sciences based on physical sense perception do not apply to the destiny of the soul and spirit after death. At this point a higher form of knowledge appears, a knowledge based on the observation of processes taking place in the soul and spirit worlds.

After freeing itself from the body, the spirit is still [19] linked to the soul. Just as the body bound it to the physical world during physical life, the soul now binds it to the soul world. But the spirit's ultimate being is not to be found in this soul world, whose purpose is only to link it to its field of activity, to the physical world. To be able to reappear in more perfected form in a new incarnation, the spirit must draw energy and strength from the spiritual world. Through the soul, however, the spirit has been entangled in the physical world, bound up with a soul being permeated and colored by physical nature, and it also took on this orientation itself.

After death, the soul is no longer bound to the body but only to the spirit. It then lives in a soul environment, and only the forces of this soul world can influence it. To begin with, the spirit is bound to the soul's life in the soul world, just as it was bound to the body during physical incarnation. The moment of the body's death is determined by the body's own laws. In general, the soul and spirit do not leave the body; it is rather dismissed by them[4] when its forces can no longer function as the human physical organization requires. The same thing applies to the relationship between soul and spirit. The soul will release the spirit into the higher world, the spiritual world, when the soul's forces no longer function as the human soul organization requires. The spirit is set free as soon as the soul surrenders to dissolution everything it can experience only in the body, and retains only what is able to live on with the spirit. This remainder, although experienced in the body, can be imprinted on the spirit as the fruits of a lifetime, and links the soul to the spirit in the purely spiritual world.

To become familiar with the soul's fate after death, we must observe the process of its dissolution. Its task had been to orient the spirit toward the physical, and as soon as this task is fulfilled, the soul itself moves in the direction of the spiritual. Because of the nature of its task, it would actually be immediately obliged to be only spiritually active once the body falls away from it and it can

---

4. Publisher's note: This passage reads, "they are rather dismissed by it" in the 19th (Stuttgart 1922) through 26th (Stuttgart 1948) editions. In all editions since the 27th (Stuttgart 1955) the wording of the 1st through 18th editions has been restored. It is not certain that the changes introduced in 1922 stem from the author, so both versions have been presented here.

no longer be a connecting link. This would happen if the soul had not been influenced by the body for a whole lifetime and had not been drawn towards the body in its own inclinations. Without the coloring it assumed through being bound up with the body, the newly disembodied soul would immediately start to obey only the laws of the spirit and soul world. This would be the case if the person in question had lost all interest in the earthly world before dying, if all the desires, wishes and so on linking that individual to the physical existence left behind had been satisfied. But to the extent that this is not the case, what remains of this orientation clings to the soul.

To avoid confusion at this point, we must clearly distinguish between something that binds a person to the world in a way that can be resolved in a future incarnation, and something that binds that individual to one particular incarnation, namely the most recent one. In the first case, the situation is resolved by karma; in the second, it can only be discarded by the soul after death.   [20]

For the human spirit, death is followed by a time in which the soul strips itself of its inclinations toward physical existence so that it can once again obey only the laws of the spirit and soul worlds and can set the spirit free. Of course this takes longer in cases where the soul has been more tightly bound to the physical. It takes little time in cases of individuals who have not been very attached to physical life, longer in cases of those whose interests were totally bound up with that life and who therefore still have many desires, wishes and so on present in their souls at death.   [21]

[22]   Gaining an idea of the state in which the soul lives during the time right after death will be easiest if we take a fairly crass example—for instance, the pleasure of a gourmet. This pleasure, of course, is not of the body but of the soul, in that both the pleasure and the desire for this pleasure belong to the soul. However, satisfying this desire requires the corresponding bodily organs—palate, taste buds and so on. After death, the soul does not immediately lose its desire, but the physical organs that used to be the means of satisfying it are no longer there. The person in question then experiences something similar to suffering from extreme thirst in an area where there is no water for miles around. (Although the reason for the suffering is different, its effects are similar but much stronger.) Because of the lack of the physical organs through which pleasure was experienced, the soul suffers burning pain at being deprived of this pleasure. The same applies to any of the soul's desires that can be satisfied only by means of physical organs. This state of burning deprivation can be called "the place of desires," although of course it is not an actual place. It lasts until the soul has learned to stop craving what can be provided only by the body.

[23]   When the soul enters the soul world after death, it is subject to the laws that prevail there, and their effects determine how the soul's inclination toward the physical will be eliminated. The effects will have to be different according to the types of soul substances and forces involved, but each type will make its cleansing and purifying influence felt. The process is such that any antipathy

in the soul is gradually overcome by the forces of sympathy, and the sympathy itself is taken to the ultimate degree. At this highest level of sympathy toward all the rest of the soul world, an individual soul merges with the rest, so to speak, becomes one with it, its self-seeking exhausted. It ceases to exist as a being inclined toward physical, sensory existence, and through this the spirit is set free. The soul undergoes purification in all the regions of the soul world described previously, until in the region of perfect sympathy it becomes one with the soul world in general.

Because the spirit has spent a lifetime in intimate association with the soul, it is bound to it until the very last moment of liberation. Having been directly linked to the soul, which was its very life, the spirit is much more closely related to it than to the body, to which it was linked only indirectly, through the soul. The spirit is bound to the soul that is gradually freeing itself, but not to the disintegrating body. Because it has a direct link to the soul, the spirit can only feel free of the soul once the soul has become one with the soul world in general.

As the human being's residence during the time immediately after death, the soul world can be called the "place of desires." The different religious systems that have incorporated an awareness of this situation into their teachings know this "place of desires" under different names such as "purgatory," "the fire of purification," and so on. [24]

The soul world's lowest region is the region of burning desire, where the soul's crudest self-serving desires, those [25] relating to the lowest aspect of bodily life, are eliminated after death. Through such desires, the soul can experience the effect of this region's forces. These forces take as their point of attack all the unfulfilled desires that remain in the soul from physical life. The sympathy in such a soul extends only to what will nourish its own self-seeking being, and is far outweighed by the antipathy in it, which pours out over anything else. However, after death its desires focus on physical pleasures that cannot possibly be satisfied in the soul world, and this impossibility intensifies its greed to the greatest possible degree. At the same time, however, this impossibility gradually extinguishes the greed. The burning lusts and desires slowly consume themselves, and the soul learns from experience that eliminating these lusts is the only way to prevent the suffering that must stem from them. During physical life such desires are repeatedly satisfied, effectively concealing the pain of burning greed behind a kind of illusion. After death, however, in the "fire of purification," this pain is fully exposed, and the corresponding deprivation must be suffered to the full.

This is indeed a dark state of affairs for the soul. Of course, only individuals whose desires focused on the coarsest things in physical life fall into this state. Those with few desires, on the other hand, have little connection to the region of burning desire and pass through it without noticing it. It must be stated that the souls spending the longest time under the influence of this region are those who became most related to its fire during physical life and therefore have the greatest need to be purified in it.

Since the soul actually longs for its own purification after death, we should not regard this purification as suffering in the sense of any comparable experience in the world of the senses. It is the only way the imperfection remaining in the soul can be eliminated.

Processes of a second type take place in the soul world, [26] processes in which sympathy and antipathy are in balance. A human soul in this condition will be influenced after death by these processes for a period of time determined by the extent to which it gave itself in life to superficial frivolities, to the pleasures of transitory sense impressions and to the influence of daily trivialities that typify this condition. People live in this condition as long as they are affected by inclinations of this sort. They let themselves be influenced by every daily triviality, but the influences fade quickly since their sympathy is not extended to any one thing in particular. Anything not belonging to this trivial realm is antipathetic to them. After death, when a soul in this condition lacks the sense-perceptible physical things needed for satisfaction, the condition must slowly die off. Naturally, the deprivation that prevails before it is fully extinguished in the soul causes suffering. In the school of this suffering, we learn to destroy the illusions in which we wrapped ourselves during physical life.

Processes of a third type in the soul world are those in [27] which sympathy and a wish-like character prevail. Our souls experience the effects of these processes through everything that maintains an atmosphere of wishing after death. This wishing, too, gradually dies off because of the impossibility of satisfying it.

[28]   The region of pleasure and displeasure in the soul world, designated above as the fourth region, subjects the soul to special trials. As long as the soul occupies a body, it takes part in everything that affects that body, such as the interweaving of pleasure and displeasure that determines the body's comfort and well-being, its discomfort and displeasure. During physical life, a human being feels the body to be the self, the basis of individual identity. The more sensuous a person's inclinations are, the more his or her feeling of identity takes on this character. After death, however, although the feeling of identity persists, the body that was its object is gone, and as a result the soul feels hollow and empty, as if it had lost itself. This lasts until the recognition dawns that the true human being is not physical in nature. Thus the effects of this fourth region destroy the illusion of the bodily self. The soul learns to no longer perceive this bodily basis as essential, and is purified and cured of its attachment to bodily existence, overcoming what used to bind it so strongly to the physical world. It can now fully unfold the forces of sympathy, which move outward. The soul has broken free from itself, as it were, and is ready to pour itself actively into the soul world in general.

[29]   At this point, we should note that suicides, having left their bodies by artificial means while the feelings bound up with their bodies remain unchanged, undergo the experiences of this region to an exceptional degree. When death is due to natural causes, the disintegration of the body is accompanied by the partial demise of the emotions that cling to it, but for suicides, in addition to the

anguish caused by feeling suddenly hollowed out, all the unsatisfied desires and wishes that prompted them to undergo disembodiment in the first place are still present.

The fifth level of the soul world is the level of soul light. Here, sympathy for others already carries considerable weight. Souls are related to this region to the extent that they took joy and pleasure in their surroundings during physical life, rather than giving themselves up to satisfying their lower needs. What undergoes purification here includes, for instance, a sensuous over-enthusiasm for nature, which must be distinguished from a loftier living-in-nature that is spiritual in character and seeks the spirit that reveals itself in the things and processes of nature. This higher feeling for nature is among the things that contribute to the development of the spirit and establish something permanent in it; this must be distinguished from a sense-based pleasure in nature which leaves the soul in need of purification as much as any other inclinations based on purely physical existence do.

Many people idealize practical arrangements that serve our sensuous well-being, such as a system of education that leads to sensuous comfort above all else. We cannot say that these people are serving only their own self-centered impulses; nevertheless, their souls are still oriented to the sense-perceptible world and must be cured of this tendency by means of the power of sympathy that prevails in the fifth region of the soul world, where any external means of satisfaction is lacking. Here, the soul gradually recognizes that this sympathy must take other

[30]

directions; sympathy for its soul surroundings must prompt the soul to pour itself out into soul space.

Those souls who expect their religious observances to enhance their sensuous well-being are also purified here, regardless of whether they yearn for an earthly or for a heavenly paradise. They find this paradise in the soul world, but only in order to recognize its worthlessness. Of course, these are all only individual examples of purifications undergone in this fifth region; many more could be added.

[31] The purification of the part of the soul that thirsts for action takes place in the sixth region, or region of active soul power. Although this action is not egotistical in character, it is still motivated by the sensuous satisfaction that it provides. The kinds of people who develop this pleasure in activity give the outward appearance of being idealists and self-sacrificing individuals, but on a deeper level they are still motivated by the heightening of sensuous pleasure. Many artistic people, as well as those who devote themselves to scientific activity for the pleasure of it, belong in this region. What binds them to the physical world is their belief that art and science exist for the sake of such pleasure.

[32] The seventh region, that of the actual soul life, frees us from our last inclinations toward the sensory, physical world. Each preceding region has absorbed that aspect of the soul that is related to it. All that is left surrounding the spirit is the belief that its activity should be totally devoted to the physical world. Many extremely gifted people think about little else than events in the physical

world; their persuasion can be called "materialism." In the seventh region, these beliefs must be and are destroyed. Our souls realize that, in actual reality, a materialistic point of view is without object, and their materialistic beliefs melt away like ice in the sun. The being of the soul is now absorbed into its own world, and the spirit, free of all restraints, wings its way upward into regions in which it lives only in its own element. The soul has completed its most recent earthly task, and in the time that has elapsed since death, any aspects of this task remaining as bonds for the spirit have dissolved. In overcoming this last earthly remnant, the soul is returned to its own element.

From what has been described, we can see that experiences in the soul world and the circumstances of soul life after death become less and less repellent as we dispose of more and more of what still clings to us from our earthly union with, and affinity for, material existence. Depending on the circumstances created during its physical life, a soul will belong to the different regions for longer or shorter periods of time. Wherever it feels an affinity, it remains until the affinity is wiped out, but where no affinity exists, it passes through without feeling any of the possible effects.

This section was intended to describe in broad strokes only the most basic features of the soul world and the nature of the soul's life within it. The same is true of the following description of the country of spirit beings. To describe further characteristics of these higher worlds would go beyond the limits of this book. Without going

[33]

into very great detail, the phenomena in these higher worlds that can be compared to spatial relationships and time spans cannot be discussed in an intelligible way, since these are all quite different from their counterparts in the physical world. Some important points on this subject are included in my *Occult Science*.[5]

III. The Country of Spirit Beings

Before we can follow the spirit as it continues its journey, [34] we must first look at the territory it is entering. This is the world of the spirit, and it is so different from the physical world that everything we have to say about it will seem sheer fantasy to those willing to trust only their physical senses. We had to use comparisons and imagery to describe the soul world, and that is even more the case here. Our language, which for the most part serves only the purposes of sense-perceptible reality, is not exactly richly endowed with expressions that can be applied directly to the "country of spirit beings," so it is especially important to take much of what is said here as nothing more than indications. Since everything described here is so different from the physical world, this is the only possible way of depicting it at all. Because of the inadequacy of our language, which is intended for communication in the physical world, the statements being made here can only

5. *An Outline of Occult Science* (Hudson, NY: Anthroposophic Press, 1972).

crudely correspond to actual experience in the spiritual field.

It must be emphasized above all that this spiritual [35] world is woven out of the substance that constitutes human thought—"substance" in a very figurative sense, of course. But thought as it appears in human beings is only a shadowy image or phantom of its real being. A thought appearing by means of a human brain corresponds to a being in the country of spirit beings as a shadow on the wall corresponds to the actual object casting the shadow. But when our spiritual senses are awakened, we actually perceive the thought being itself, just as our physical eyes perceive a table or a chair. We are surrounded and accompanied by thought beings. Our physical eyes perceive a lion, and our sense-oriented thinking perceives the idea of the lion merely as a phantom, a shadowy image. But in the country of spirit beings, the idea of the lion is as real and visible to our spiritual eyes as the physical lion is to our physical eyes. The comparison we used in connection with the soul world is also pertinent. Just as people who were born blind but have had their sight restored through operations suddenly perceive their surroundings as having the new qualities of color and light, those who have learned to use their spiritual eyes perceive their surroundings as filled with a whole new world of *living* thoughts or spirit beings.

The first things to be seen in this world are the spiritual *archetypes* of all the things and beings that exist in the physical and soul worlds. If you imagine a painting as existing in the spiritual world before the artist paints it, you will have an image of what is meant by the term "archetype." That the painter may not have this archetype in mind before starting to paint, that he may only come to it gradually as the painting is actually being worked on, is beside the point. In the spiritual world, these archetypes exist for all things; physical things and beings are copies or imitations of their archetypes. Quite understandably, people who trust only their outer senses will deny the existence of this archetypal world and insist that archetypes are only abstractions that the intellect works out by comparing sense-perceptible things. Such people cannot perceive at all in this higher world; they are aware of the world of thoughts only in its shadowy abstractness. They do not know that individuals capable of spiritual vision are as familiar with spirit beings as they themselves are with their dogs or cats, and that the reality of the archetypal world is actually much more intense than physical sense-perceptible reality.

[36]   It is true that looking into this country of spirit beings for the first time is even more confusing than looking into the soul world, because archetypes in their true forms are very unlike their sense-perceptible copies, and they bear equally little resemblance to their "shadows," our abstract thoughts. In the spiritual world, everything is in constant activity, constant motion, constant creation. "Resting" or "staying in one place" does not exist there as it does in the physical world, simply because the archetypes are creative beings, the master builders of everything that comes into existence in the physical and soul worlds. Their forms change quickly, and each archetype

has the potential to assume countless specific forms.[6] It is as if the specialized forms well up out of them—one form has hardly been created before its archetype is ready to let the next one pour out. In addition, archetypes do not work alone, but stand in closer or more distant relationship to each other. One archetype may need the help of another to do its creating, and often innumerable archetypes work together so that some particular being can come to life in the soul world or the physical world.

In addition to what can be perceived by means of spiritual "sight" in the country of spirit beings, the experience of spiritual "hearing" must also be taken into account, for as soon as a clairvoyant ascends from the soul world into the spirit, the archetypes also begin to resound. This resounding is a purely spiritual process that must be conceived of without any thought of physical sound. To an observer, it is like being in an ocean of sounds and tones in which the beings of the spiritual world are expressing themselves. Their interrelationships and the archetypal laws of their existence reveal themselves in the chords, harmonies, rhythms and melodies of this spiritual "music," which reveals to our spiritual "ear" what reasoning

[37]

---

6. Although it is true that "[t]here is no such thing [in the spiritual world] as 'resting' or 'staying in one place' as there is in the physical world[,]" it would be incorrect to assume that the spiritual world is a place of constant unrest. In this world where "the archetypes are creative beings," although there is nothing that can be called "resting in one place," there is a peace of a spiritual kind that is totally compatible with active mobility. The spiritual equivalent of "rest" is peaceful contentment and bliss manifesting in activity rather than inactivity.

in the physical world perceives as an idea or natural law. Hence the Pythagoreans called this perception of the spiritual world "the music of the spheres." To those with functioning spiritual ears, this music of the spheres is no symbol or allegory but a familiar spiritual reality. To acquire an idea of this spiritual music, we must dispense with all our sensory concepts of music as we perceive it by means of our material ears. Spiritual perception is involved here, perception of a sort that remains silent for the physical ear.

For simplicity's sake, all references to "spiritual music" will be omitted in the following descriptions of the country of spirit beings. We must imagine, however, that everything described as an image, as "shining" or "radiant," is also "sounding." Every color, every sensation of light, corresponds to a spiritual tone; every interaction among colors corresponds to a harmony or a melody, and so on. We must keep in mind that spiritual seeing does not cease where spiritual sound prevails; the sounding simply augments the radiance. And where archetypes or archetypal images are mentioned, we need to imagine primal tones as well. Other modes of perception that could be called "spiritual tasting," and so on, are also involved, but we will not go into these processes now since the point is simply to alert us to a conception of the spiritual world, taking certain modes of perception as examples.

[38]   First of all, we need to be able to distinguish between different kinds of archetypes. Here in the country of spirit beings, as in the soul world, there are a number of different levels or regions that we must be able to differentiate in

order to orient ourselves. Here, too, these individual regions are to be imagined as if interpenetrating rather than layered or piled on top of one another. The first region contains the archetypes of things in the physical world that are not endowed with life. The archetypes of minerals are to be found here, and those of plants, but only to the extent that they are purely physical, that is, to the extent that we do not take their inherent life into account. In the same way, we also find the physical forms of animals and human beings here. This is not an exhaustive list of what is to be found in this first region, but only a few illustrative examples.

This region constitutes the basic structure of the country of spirit beings, and can be compared to the solid land masses of our physical earth. It is the continental mass of this spirit country. Of course, its relationship to the physical bodily world can be described only by means of comparisons. We can get some idea of it as follows: Imagine a finite space filled with a wide variety of physical bodies, then imagine that the physical bodies are gone and visualize hollow spaces of the same shapes in their places. Imagine that what used to be the empty spaces between the bodies is filled with a wide variety of forms that relate to the former bodies in many different ways. This is somewhat similar to how things appear in the lowest region of the world of archetypes: Things and beings that are embodied in the physical world exist as hollow spaces here, and the mobile activity of the archetypes and the spiritual music goes on in between them. When the time comes for physical embodiment, the hollow spaces are then filled in with matter, so to speak. Anyone looking into space with both physical and spiritual eyes would see physical bodies, and among them the mobile activity of the creative archetypes.

The second region of the country of spirit beings contains the archetypes of life, but here this life forms a perfect unity. It streams through the spiritual world like a fluid element, and is similar to blood in how it pulses through everything. It could be likened to the physical world's oceans and other bodies of water, although its distribution more closely resembles that of the blood in animal bodies than that of oceans and rivers. This second level of the country of spirit beings might be described as "flowing life formed from thought substance." In this element are the creative archetypal forces for everything that appears in physical reality as enlivened being. It is apparent here that all life is a unity, that the life within us as human beings is related to the life of all our fellow creatures.

[39]   The archetypes of everything of a soul nature make up the third region of the country of spirit beings. Here we are in a much thinner and finer element than in the first two regions, in an element that can be described, figuratively speaking, as the "atmosphere" of this country of spirit beings. Everything taking place in souls in the two other worlds has its spiritual counterpart here; all sensations, feelings, instincts, passions and so on are also present here once again, but in spiritual form. The atmospheric processes taking place in this "air" correspond to the sorrows and joys of creatures in the other worlds—the longing of a human soul appears as a light breeze, a passionate outbreak as a stormy blast. Those capable of visualizing what is going on here can penetrate deeply into the

sighs of any ensouled being if they turn their attention to it. Here, for example, we can talk about thunderstorms with flashing lightning and rolling thunder; if we pursue the matter further, we find that these spiritual storms express the passions of battles being fought on earth.

The archetypes of the fourth region do not relate directly to the other worlds. In a certain respect, these archetypes are beings that govern the archetypes of the three lower regions and mediate their coming together, ordering and grouping them. It follows that the activity proceeding from this region is more encompassing than that of the lower regions.   *[40]*

The fifth, sixth and seventh regions are fundamentally different from the previous ones because the beings at home in them provide the archetypes of the lower regions with the impulses required for their activity. There the creative forces of the archetypes themselves are to be found. When we can ascend as high as these three regions, we become acquainted with the "intentions"[7] underlying   *[41]*

---

7. Terms like "intention" are used here in a metaphorical sense, as will be obvious from previous discussion of the difficulties involved in expressing these things through language. Reviving the old teleological "doctrine of purpose" is not what is intended. The terms "purposes" and "intentions" must be used here with regard to the driving forces behind world evolution, even though this makes it tempting to misinterpret these powers in terms of purposes or intentions on the human level. This temptation can be avoided only by raising these words to a new level of meaning where they can be free of anything that would restrict them to the merely human level and can assume a meaning we human beings approach in those moments in our lives when we transcend ourselves to a certain extent.

our world. The archetypes lie ready here like germinal points of life, waiting to assume the various forms of thought beings. When these germinal points are projected into the lower regions, they immediately well up and manifest in the most varied forms. The ideas through which the human spirit appears creatively in the physical world are reflections or shadows of these germinal thought beings of the higher spiritual world. On ascending from the lower regions of spirit country to these upper ones, observers possessing the "spiritual ear" become aware that sounds and tones are transformed into spiritual language; they begin to perceive the "spiritual word" through which objects and beings communicate their nature not only in music but also in words, speaking out what can be called in spiritual science their "eternal names."[8]

[42]   We must imagine these germinal thought beings as composite in nature. Only the germ sheath, which surrounds the actual life kernel of these beings, is taken from the elements of the world of thoughts. At this point, we arrive at the limits of the three worlds, since the life kernel itself has its origin in still higher worlds. When in an earlier chapter we considered the human being as made up of various component members, this life kernel was described and its parts called the "life spirit" and "spirit body." Other cosmic beings also have similar life kernels that originate in higher worlds and are moved into the three we have discussed in order to perform their tasks there.

---

8. *Occult Science* contains more on the subject of the spiritual word.

At this juncture, we will follow the human spirit as it continues its pilgrimage through spirit country between two incarnations or embodiments. As we do so, the circumstances and distinctive characteristics of this country will once again become clear to us.

IV. The Spirit in Spirit Country after Death

Once a human spirit has passed through the world of souls on its journey between two incarnations, it enters the country of spirits, where it remains until it is ready for a new bodily existence. We can understand the meaning of this stay in spirit country only if we are able to interpret properly the purpose of our life's pilgrimage in an incarnation. While we are incarnated in physical bodies, we human beings work and create in the physical world, but we work and create as *spiritual* beings. What we imprint on physical forms, materials and forces our spirits think out and develop. Our task as messengers of the spiritual world is to incorporate the spirit into the material world. Only through incarnating in physical bodies can we work in the material world. We must take on physical bodies as our tools so that we have something material through which to work on the material world and through which the material world can work on us. However, what works through our human bodily nature is the *spirit*. The intentions and directions for our work in the material world come from the spirit.

[43]

As long as the spirit is active in a physical body, it cannot work in its true form as spirit, but can only shine through the veil of physical existence, so to speak. In reality, our human thought life belongs to the spiritual world, but as it appears within our physical existence its true form is veiled. We might also say that the thought activity of physical human beings is a shadowy image, a reflection, of the true spiritual being to which it belongs. During physical life, the spirit interacts with the earthly material world by using a material body as its basis.

It is true that one of the tasks of the human spirit, as long as this spirit is proceeding from incarnation to incarnation, is to work in the physical world, but this task could not be completed appropriately if the spirit lived only an embodied existence. The intentions and goals of an earthly task are no more worked out and determined within an earthly incarnation than the blueprint for a building comes about on the site where the builders are already at work. The plan for the building is worked out in the architect's office, and the goals and intentions of earthly endeavor are developed in the country of spirits, where each human spirit must dwell again and again between incarnations in order to equip itself for work in a physical lifetime. The architect draws up the plan for a house in the office, according to architectural and other standards, and does this without touching actual bricks and mortar. Similarly, the architect of human creativity—the spirit or higher self—develops the necessary goals and capabilities according to the laws of the country of spirit beings, in order to then send them into the earthly world. Only by returning again and again to its own realm will a human spirit be able to bring the spirit into the earthly world by means of its physical-material instrument.

In the physical arena, we learn to know the characteristics and forces of the physical world; while working, we gather experience about what the physical world requires of those who want to work in it. We also learn to know the characteristics of the matter we intend to use to embody our thoughts and ideas, although these ideas and thoughts themselves cannot be derived from matter. Thus the physical world is the setting for both work and learning. Afterwards, in spirit country, what has been learned is transformed into the active abilities and capacities of the human spirit.

To make things clearer, the comparison we used above can be taken further. An architect works out a design for a house, and this plan is carried out. In the process, the architect gains experience in a number of ways so that his or her capabilities are enhanced. When the next design has to be drawn up, all these experiences flow into it. The second design is enriched by everything learned in the process of carrying out the first. It is the same with successive human lifetimes. In the intervals between incarnations, the spirit is at home in its own realm and is able to devote itself totally to the requirements of spiritual life. Released from physical existence, it develops in all directions and incorporates the fruits of its experience in previous lifetimes into this process. Its attention is thus always directed to the earthly context of its tasks. To the extent that the earth is the spirit's field of action, the spirit is constantly working to keep pace with the earth's evolution, and is working on itself so that in each incarnation the service it performs corresponds to the earth's situation at that time. Of course, this is only a very general picture of successive human lifetimes; reality never conforms totally to this picture but only approximates it. Circumstances can dictate that a person's next life is much less perfect than the preceding one, but on the whole these irregularities are balanced out within precise limits in successive incarnations.

[44]   The course of our spirit's development in the country of spirit beings takes place through our becoming fully involved in the life of each of its different regions. Our own life dissolves into each region in succession; we temporarily assume the characteristics of each of these regions. As a result, their being permeates our being so that we are strengthened in our work on earth.

In the first region of the country of spirit beings, we are surrounded by the spiritual archetypes of earthly things. During an earthly lifetime, we only learn to know the shadows of these archetypes, which we grasp in our own thoughts. What is merely *thought* on earth is *experienced* in this region. We are surrounded by thoughts as we proceed on our way, but these thoughts are *real beings*. What we perceived through our senses during earthly life now works on us in its thought form, but the thought appears to us, not as a shadow hiding behind the things, but as a living reality that creates the things. We are in the thought workshop, so to speak, where earthly things are shaped and formed. Everything in the country of spirits is full of lively activity and movement. Here the thought world is at work as a world of living beings, creating and forming; we see here how what we experienced during earthly existence is shaped and formed. In our physical bodies we experienced sense-perceptible things as realities, but now, as spirits, we experience spiritual formative forces as real.

Also present among the thought beings here is the idea of our own physical, bodily nature, from which we now feel quite removed; we experience only our spiritual being as actually belonging to us. When we do become aware, as if in memory, of the body we have laid aside, we see it no longer as a physical being but rather as a thought being, and then the fact that it belongs to the outer world becomes a direct observation. We learn to regard it as something belonging to the outer world, as an extension of the outer world. As a result, we no longer consider our own physical existence to be more closely related to ourselves, so we cease to separate it from the rest of the world. We experience the entire outer world, including our own physical embodiments, as a unity; our personal physical embodiments merge into a unity with the rest of the world. At this stage, we view the archetypes of physical, bodily reality as a unity to which we ourselves once belonged. Through observation, we gradually learn to recognize our relationship to, our unity with, our surroundings, to realize that we ourselves once were what is spread out around us here.

This is one of the fundamental ideas of ancient Indian Vedanta wisdom. The sage acquires during earthly life what other people experience only after death, namely the ability to grasp the thought that we ourselves are related to all things, the thought, "that is you." In earthly life this is an ideal that our thinking can aspire to, but in the country of spirit beings it is an immediate fact that becomes ever clearer as we gain spiritual experience. We become ever more aware that, in our essential being, we belong to the spiritual world. We perceive ourselves as spirits among spirits, as organs of the primal spirits. We feel in ourselves their word, "I am the primal spirit," or, in terms of Vedanta wisdom, "I am Brahman," that is, I am part of, an organ of, the primal being from which all beings spring. Thus we see that what we grasp during earthly life as a shadowy idea and the object of all wisdom's aspiration is a matter of direct experience in the spirit world. This idea can be thought during earthly life only because it is an actual fact in spiritual existence.

[45]   During spiritual existence, we see the relationships and circumstances that surrounded us during earthly life from a more elevated vantage point, as if from outside. While we live in the spirit country's lowest region, this is how we relate to earthly circumstances having to do directly with physical, bodily reality. We are born on earth into a family and an ethnic group, and we live in a particular country. All these circumstances determine our earthly existence. We find that the circumstances in the physical world cause us to become friends with particular people or to pursue a particular line of work; they determine the general character of our life. In the first region of the

country of spirit beings, all this confronts us as a living thought-entity. In a certain sense, we live through it all again, but from the active spiritual side. Our love for our family and the friendship we extended to others are now enlivened in us from within, and our capacities in this direction are enhanced. What works in the human spirit as the force of love of family and friends is strengthened, and in this respect, we later enter earthly existence as more perfected human beings. For the most part, our daily relationships in earthly life are what ripen into fruit in this lowest region of the country of spirit beings. The aspect of the human being that in its interests is wholly bound up with these daily circumstances will feel related to this region for the greatest portion of the spiritual life between incarnations.

The people with whom we lived in the physical world are encountered again in the spiritual world. Just as everything that the soul once possessed through the physical body falls away, so does the bond that once linked soul to soul in physical life free itself from the circumstances that only had meaning and reality in the physical world. But what one soul was to another in physical life lives on after death, lives on in the spiritual world. Of course words coined to describe physical circumstances can only inexactly express what takes place in the spiritual world. Taking this into account, however, it is certainly correct to say that souls who belonged together during physical life meet again in the spiritual world and continue their lives together under the circumstances of that world.

The next region is the one in which the life that is common to the thought being of the entire earthly world flows and streams as the fluid element of the spiritual world, so to speak. As long as we are observing the world from the vantage point of physical embodiment, life appears bound to individual living things. In the country of spirit beings, however, life is released from individual things and flows throughout like the blood of life, as a living unity that is present in all things. During earthly life we get only a glimmer or a reflection of this, which is expressed in any devotion we bring toward the whole, toward the unity and harmony of the world. Our religious life derives from this reflection, making us aware of the extent to which the comprehensive meaning of existence does *not* lie in anything individual and transitory. We come to regard transitory existence as an image or likeness of something eternal, of a harmonious whole, and we look up to this unity reverently and worshipfully in performing our religious rituals. In the country of spirit beings, however, living thought nature appears in its true form rather than as a reflection, and we can actually unite with the unity we worshiped on earth. Our religious life and everything related to it bears fruit in this region. Here, spiritual experience teaches us that our individual destinies cannot be separated from the community to which we belong, and the ability to recognize ourselves as parts of a whole develops. Religious feeling and everything in us that struggled for pure and noble morality during our lifetime will draw strength from this region during the greater part of the interval we spend in it, and we are then reembodied with our abilities enhanced in this regard.

In the first region, we were in the company of the souls [46] to whom we were most closely linked in the physical world in our previous lifetime. In the second region, we come into the presence of all those with whom we felt united in a wider sense through a common devotion, a common faith and so on. It must be emphasized that our spiritual experiences in preceding regions continue in the next, so we are not torn out of the context of family, friends and so on when we take part in the life of the second and successive regions. The regions of the country of spirit beings are not separate "departments"; they interpenetrate each other. We experience being in a new region not because we have "entered" it in any outward way, but because we have only now acquired the inner ability to perceive something that has been surrounding us all the time.

The third region of the country of spirit beings contains [47] the archetypes of the soul world. Everything that lives in that world is present here as a living thought being; we find here the archetypes of desires, wishes, emotions and so on. But no self-seeking clings to the soul here in the spirit world. Just as all life constitutes a unity in the second region, all desires, wishes, pleasures and displeasures form a unity in this third region, so that what others wish and desire is indistinguishable from what I wish and desire. The sensations and feelings of all beings form a common world that encloses and surrounds everything else, like the air that surrounds the earth. This region is, so to speak, the "atmosphere" of the country of spirit beings. Everything done during earthly life in the service of the common good and in selfless devotion to our fellow human beings will bear fruit here in this third region, because by living in service and devotion we were already living in its reflection. Humankind's great benefactors, devoted individuals who perform great services for their communities, acquired their ability to do so in this region after having prepared themselves for a special relationship to it in earlier lifetimes.

[48]   Obviously, the three regions of spirit country that have been described so far relate in a particular way to the worlds below, to the physical and soul worlds, in that they contain the archetypes or living thought beings that assume physical or soul existence in the other two worlds. The fourth region is the first that is pure spirit country, although not in the fullest sense of the word. It differs from the three lower regions in that they contain the archetypes of things and beings we find as "givens" before we ourselves intervene in these worlds. Our everyday life on earth is related to these transient things, which, however, direct our attention to their basis in eternity. These transient things, and also our fellow creatures to whom we turn our selfless attention, are not there because of us. But what is in the world because of us is everything created through the arts and sciences, through technology, the state and so on—everything we incorporate into the world as original works of our spirit. Without our participation, no image of these things would exist in the world. The archetypes for these purely

human creations are to be found in the fourth region of the country of spirit beings. Everything human beings develop during earthly life by way of scientific accomplishments, artistic ideas and forms, and technological thinking bears fruit in this fourth region. Artists, scholars and great inventors draw their impulses from this region during their stay in the spirit world; here their genius is enhanced so that during later incarnations they can contribute still more to the further development of our civilization.

But we must not imagine that this fourth region is of significance for outstanding individuals only; it is of significance for all of us. Any concerns during physical life that transcend the sphere of mundane activity, wishes and desires have their ultimate source in this region. If we spent the interval between death and a new birth without passing through this region, in the next life we would have no interests reaching beyond the narrow circumference of our own personal life to universal human concerns. As it has just been said, not even this region can be called "pure spirit country" in the fullest sense of the word, because the condition in which we have left the earth's cultural development plays into our spiritual existence in this region. In the spiritual world we can enjoy only the fruits of whatever our own talents and the degree of development of our ethnic group, nation and so on have allowed us to achieve.

In the still higher regions of the country of spirit beings, [49] the human spirit is relieved of all earthly bonds and ascends to a purely spiritual world, where it experiences the intentions and goals it established for earthly life. Everything that is actually achieved in the world brings these highest goals and intentions into existence only in the form of a relatively feeble copy. Every crystal, every tree, every animal, and also everything we accomplish through our own creativity—all these provide only copies of what the spirit intended. During our incarnations, all we can do is link up with these imperfect copies of perfect intentions and goals. We ourselves can only be copies or imitations of what the kingdom of the spirit intended us to be. Therefore, what we actually are as spirits in the country of spirit beings is only evident once we have reached the fifth region of spirit country during the interval between two incarnations. Here we are really ourselves; we are what assumes outer existence in our various incarnations. In this region our true human self, the self that appears anew in each incarnation, can come to full expression. Since it brings with it abilities that have matured in the spirit world's lower regions, it carries the fruits of earlier lifetimes over into succeeding ones. It is the vehicle for the results of earlier incarnations.

[50]   When the self is in the fifth region of the country of spirit beings, it dwells in the kingdom of intentions and goals. In the fifth region, like an architect who learns from imperfections that have become evident and who includes in future designs only what he or she has been able to perfect, the self discards any of the results of experience in earlier lifetimes that have to do with lower-worldly imperfections. It is now at home with the intentions of the country of spirit beings and fructifies them

with the results of earlier lifetimes. Clearly, the strength that can be drawn from this region depends on the extent to which the embodied self has achieved results that are fit to be taken up into the world of intentions. A self that has attempted to realize the intentions of the spirit by means of its active thought life or wise and loving work during earthly life will be a good candidate for this region. On the other hand, nothing that is totally given over to mundane circumstances, nothing that dwells on and in transitory things, can sow seeds capable of playing any role in the purposes of the eternal order of the world. Only those few things that have had an effect extending beyond everyday interests can develop into fruit in these upper regions of the country of spirit beings.

However, we must not imagine that worldly renown or any such thing is what is meant here. It is rather a question of anything, even in the most restrictive life situation, that leads to an awareness of each single thing's importance in the eternal progressive course of existence. In this region, we must become accustomed to assessing things differently than we are able to do in physical life. For instance, if we have acquired very little that relates to this fifth region, we feel an urgent need to imprint on ourselves an impulse that will cause our next life to run its course in such a way that the *effect* of this deficit becomes apparent in the destiny or karma we meet. The "unfortunate fate"—to put it in terms of that lifetime—that meets us there, and that may even provoke bitter complaining, appears in the fifth region as exactly what we need. Since in this fifth region we are dwelling in our true self, we are raised above everything lower-worldly that enveloped us during our incarnations. Here, we are what we always have been and always will be in the course of our incarnations. We are living under the authority of the intentions that exist for these incarnations, intentions that we incorporate into our own self. That is, we look back on our past and are aware that everything we have experienced is being absorbed into intentions that we will have to realize in future. A certain capacity to remember earlier lifetimes as well as a prophetic preview of later ones flares up. We know that what this book calls the "spirit self," to the extent that it is already developed, is in its own element in this region, where it continues to develop and prepares itself to be able to fulfill spiritual intentions in earthly reality in a new incarnation.

[51]   If, through a series of sojourns in the country of spirit beings, this "spirit self" has developed to the point where it can move about totally freely there, it will seek its true home there more and more in times to come. Life in the spirit becomes as familiar to it as life in physical reality is to earthly human beings. At this stage of development, the viewpoint of the spiritual world begins to prevail as the one the self chooses more or less consciously as the standard for its earthly lives to come. It feels itself to be a member of the world's divine order, and the laws and limitations of earthly life do not touch its innermost being. The strength needed for everything that it carries out comes from the spiritual world. But this spiritual world is a unity, and those who live in it know that the eternal has worked to create the past. They are also able to determine

their future direction in accordance with the eternal; their view, once restricted to the past, has expanded and become perfect.[9] Human beings who have reached this level provide for themselves the goals they are to achieve in their next incarnation. Working out of the country of spirit beings, such human beings influence their own future so that it proceeds in line with what is true and spiritual. Because they have climbed to the level where they can understand divine wisdom, these human beings spend the intervals between incarnations in the presence of all the exalted beings who have an unrestricted view of that wisdom.

---

9. The statement that "[t]hey are also able to determine their future direction in accordance with the eternal[,]" is intended to point to the special character of the soul's constitution during the time between death and a new birth. By the standards of life in the physical world, a stroke of destiny in the life of an individual may seem to be in direct conflict with what that person wants and intends. During life between death and birth, however, a will-like force that prevails in the human soul points the way for the person in question to experience that very blow of fate. The soul perceives, as it were, an imperfection clinging to it from previous earthly lives as a result of some ugly deed or thought. During the interval between death and birth, a will-like impulse that arises in the soul urges it to balance out this imperfection. As a result, the soul acquires the tendency to plunge into some misfortune in its subsequent earthly life, something it must suffer in order to restore equilibrium. Once it has been born into a physical body and hit by this stroke of destiny, the soul in question has no inkling that in its pre-birth life in the spirit it had actively pushed itself in the direction of this hard fate, but in actual fact—as unwished for and unintended as this blow may seem from the viewpoint of earthly life—the soul has willed it upon itself in the course of its supersensible existence. "Out of eternity, human beings determine their future."

In the sixth region of the country of spirit beings, everything that human beings do brings about what is best suited to the true and essential nature of the world. Human beings can no longer seek what is to their own advantage, but only what should happen according to the proper progression of the world order.

The seventh region of the spirit world leads to the boundary of the three worlds we have discussed. Here, human beings stand face to face with the "kernels of life" that are transplanted from still higher worlds into these three where they will complete their tasks. Having arrived at the limits of the three worlds, human beings recognize themselves in their own "kernels of life." This means that the riddles of these three worlds have been solved for them; they have acquired a full overview of the life in these worlds. Under ordinary circumstances in physical life, the soul faculties by which we experience the spiritual world in the way described here do not become conscious. They work in unconscious depths on the physical organs to bring about consciousness in the physical world, and thus they remain imperceptible as far as this world is concerned. An eye, too, is incapable of seeing itself because the forces that make it possible to see other things are at work in it. If we want to assess the extent to which a human life between birth and death is the result of earlier earthly lives, we must take into account the fact that a vantage point situated within this life itself does not allow us to do so. From this point of view, an earthly life might appear to be imperfect, full of suffering and so on, while to a point of view based outside earthly life, the form this life assumes in all its suffering and imperfection would prove to be the consequence of earlier lives. By setting out on the path to knowledge as it is described in a subsequent chapter of this book, the soul can free itself from the circumstances of bodily life and perceive an image of the experiences it undergoes between death and a new birth. This type of perception makes it possible to depict the processes taking place in the spirit world, as has been done here in a sketchy form. Only when we remember that the soul's entire constitution is different in the physical body than it is when it is undergoing purely spiritual experiences, can we see these depictions in the right light.

V. The Physical World and its Connection to the Worlds of Souls and Spirits

The formations of the soul and spirit worlds cannot be the object of outer sensory perception. Sense-perceptible objects must be reckoned as a third world alongside the other two. During bodily existence, we live in all three worlds at once: We perceive the objects of the sense-perceptible world and work on them. Soul structures work on us through their forces of sympathy and antipathy, while we ourselves stir up waves in the soul world with our likes and dislikes, wishes and desires. The spiritual nature of things, however, is reflected in our thought world, and as thinking spirit beings we are citizens of the country of spirit beings and comrades of everything that lives in this realm.

[52]

This makes it clear that the sense-perceptible world is only part of what surrounds us. It is distinct from, and to a certain extent independent of, our overall surroundings simply because it can be perceived with senses that disregard the soul and spiritual aspects of these surroundings. It is like a piece of ice floating on water—the ice consists of the same substance as the surrounding water but stands out because of certain qualities it possesses. In the same way, sense-perceptible things are of the same substance as the soul and spirit worlds surrounding them, but they stand out because of certain characteristics that make them perceptible to our senses. To put it somewhat figuratively, they are condensed spirit and soul formations, and the condensation makes it possible for our senses to acquire knowledge about them. Ice is just one of the manifestations of water, and sense-perceptible things are just one form in which soul and spirit beings exist. Having grasped this, we can also understand that the spirit world can change into the soul world and the soul world into the sensory world, just as water can turn to ice.

[53]   From this perspective, it also becomes clear why we human beings are able to think thoughts about sense-perceptible things. Every thinking person must ask the question, "What is the relationship of my thoughts about a stone to the stone itself?" For people who are able to look into nature especially deeply, this question appears clearly to their mind's eye; they experience the world of human thoughts as being in harmony with the structure and order of nature. Kepler, the famous astronomer, put it very beautifully:

The truth is that the divine calling that bids us study astronomy is inscribed on the world itself, not in words and syllables but in the very fact that our human concepts and senses are adapted to perceive how heavenly bodies, heavenly circumstances, are linked.[10]

Only because sense-perceptible things are nothing other than condensed spirit beings can we human beings—who can lift ourselves up in thought to the level of spirit beings—think about and understand them. Sense-perceptible things originate in the spirit world and are simply another manifestation of spirit beings; when we formulate thoughts about things, we are simply inwardly directed away from their sense-perceptible forms and toward their spiritual archetypes. Understanding an object by thinking about it is a process that can be compared to melting a solid body so that chemists can study it in its fluid form.

The spiritual archetypes of the sense-perceptible world *[54]* are to be found in the different regions of spirit country. In the fifth, sixth, and seventh regions, they still exist as living germinal points, while in the four lower regions they take shape as spiritual formations. When the human spirit tries to come to an understanding of sense-perceptible objects by means of thinking, it perceives shadowy copies or imitations of spiritual formations. In aspiring to

---

10. Johannes Kepler, 1571-1630. This passage is from the "Commentaries" on his book *Astronomia Nova*, Part II, Chapter VII.

a spiritual understanding of our surroundings, we raise the question of how spiritual formations condense into sense-perceptibility.

To our sensory perception, the world around us is divided into four clearly distinguishable levels, the mineral, plant, animal and human levels. The mineral kingdom is perceived by means of the senses and understood by means of thinking. When we formulate a thought about a mineral object, we are dealing with two things, the sense-perceptible object and the thought. Accordingly, we must imagine this sense-perceptible thing as a condensed thought being. Now, one mineral entity acts outwardly on another; it bumps into it and makes it move, warms it, illuminates it, dissolves it, and so on. This outward way of working can be expressed in thoughts. In the process of having thoughts about how mineral objects influence each other in a regular and lawful manner, our isolated thoughts expand into a thought image of the whole mineral world. This thought image is a reflection of the archetype of the entire mineral sense-perceptible world, and can be found *as a whole* in the spiritual world.

In the plant kingdom, the phenomena of growth and reproduction are added to the fact that one thing outwardly affects another. Plants grow and produce beings of the same kind, so *life* is added to what we encounter in the mineral kingdom. Simply pondering this state of affairs will lead us to a point of view that sheds light on the subject. Each plant possesses the inherent power to create its own living form and to pass it on to a being of its own kind. The forms of crystals stand midway between mineral substances of the formless sort, such as those we encounter in gases, liquids, and so on, and the living forms of the plant world. In crystals we find the transition from the formless mineral world to the living capacity of the plant kingdom to produce forms. The outward sense-perceptible process of assuming shape, as it takes place in both the mineral and plant kingdoms, must be seen as a sense-perceptible condensation of a purely spiritual process that occurs when the spiritual germinal points of the three upper regions of the country of spirit beings develop into the spirit formations of the lower regions. The spiritual archetype of crystallization is the transition from a formless spirit germ point to a spiritual formation with a shape. If this transitional process condenses to the point where our senses can perceive its result, it manifests in the sense-perceptible world as the process of mineral crystallization.

In the plant world, too, a spirit germ that has assumed form is present, but in this case the formed being retains the living sculptural ability that the crystal's spirit germ lost when it took on shape, exhausting its life in the formation it produced. In contrast, plants possess both form and the ability to go on forming; this characteristic of spirit germs is retained from the spiritual world's upper regions. Thus, a plant is both form, like the crystal, and formative force. In addition to the form that archetypal beings assume in the shape of a plant, the plant is also worked upon by another form that bears the imprint of spirit beings from the upper regions. However, the only aspect of the plant that is sense-perceptible is what expresses itself in the completed form; the formative beings that give this form its life are present within the plant kingdom without being perceptible to our senses. Our physical eyes can see a lily that is first small, then larger, but they cannot see the sculpting force that makes it grow. This sculpting force-being is the invisibly active component of the plant kingdom. Spirit germs have stepped down one level in order to work in the realm of formations. If we call the archetypal forms that have not assumed specific shape the *first elemental kingdom*, then the force-beings that are invisible to our senses and that work at sculpting the growth of plants belong to the *second elemental kingdom*.

In the animal world, the ability to grow and reproduce is augmented by sensations and impulses. These are manifestations of the soul world. Any being endowed with them belongs to the soul world, receives impressions from it and exerts an influence on it. Now, every sensation or impulse that comes about in an animal is brought up from the depths of the animal's soul. However, the animal's form is more lasting than these sensations or impulses. We might say that the animal's sentient activity compares to its more permanent enlivened form as the changeable form of a plant compares to the fixed form of a crystal. The plant, so to speak, is totally taken up with the force that sculpts forms. It continues to incorporate different forms throughout its life as it produces first roots, then leaves, then flowers, and so on. In contrast, the animal has a finished form within which it develops an ever-changing life of sensations and impulses. This life exists in the soul world. Plants grow and reproduce, while animals perceive, feel, and develop impulses. For the animal, these impulses are something formless that evolves through ever new forms. Ultimately, the archetypal processes of these impulses are to be found in the highest regions of the country of spirit beings, but they are active and at work in the soul world.

In animals, then, in addition to the force-beings invisibly at work directing growth and reproduction, others are also present that have descended one stage deeper into the soul world. In the animal kingdom, sensations and impulses are crafted by formless beings that slip into soul garments. These are the actual architects of animal forms. In spiritual science, the realm to which they belong can be called the *third elemental kingdom.*

We human beings are equipped not only with the capabilities characteristic of plants and animals, but also with the ability to develop sensations into concepts and thoughts and to govern our impulses with thinking. Thought, which appears as form in plants and as soul faculties in animals, appears in human beings in its real form, as thought itself. Animals are soul; human beings are spirit. The spirit being shapes the soul in an animal; in a human being, it descends one step further into the sense-perceptible world of matter itself. The spirit is present in sense-perceptible garb within the physical human body and can thus appear only as a spirit being's shadowy reflection as thought represents it. The spirit appears within a human being under conditions imposed by the physical organization of the human brain. However, it also becomes the inner being of a human individual.

In human beings, the form assumed by the formless spirit being is thought, while in plants it assumes the guise of form and in animals, that of the soul. Therefore, to the extent that we humans are thinking beings, there is no elemental kingdom building us up from outside. Our elemental kingdom works in our sense-perceptible body, and only to the extent that we are formed and sentient beings do the elemental beings work on us in the way they work on plants and animals. Our thought organization, however, is worked on only from within our physical body. In our spiritual organs, in our nervous system which culminates in a perfected brain, we are confronted in sense-perceptible form with what works imperceptibly, as a force-being, on plants and animals. This means that animals *feel* themselves, but human beings are *conscious* of themselves. In animals, the spirit experiences itself as soul but does not yet grasp itself as spirit. In human beings, however, the spirit recognizes itself as such, although physical circumstances permit it to appear only as a shadowy reflection of the spirit, as thought.

Accordingly, the threefold world falls into the following subdivisions:

I. The kingdom of archetypal formless beings (first elemental kingdom);

II. The kingdom of form-creating beings (second elemental kingdom);

III. The kingdom of soul beings (third elemental kingdom);

IV. The kingdom of created forms (crystal forms);

V. The kingdom of sense-perceptible forms worked on by the form-creating beings (plant kingdom);

VI. The kingdom of sense-perceptible forms worked on by both the form-creating beings and the beings that express themselves as soul (animal kingdom);

VIII. The kingdom of sense-perceptible forms worked on by form-creating and soul beings, and in which the spirit appears in the sense-perceptible world in the form of thought (human kingdom).

This demonstrates how the constitutional components [55] of an embodied human being relate to the spiritual world. Physical body, ether body, sentient soul body and mind soul are to be regarded as condensations in the sense-perceptible world of archetypes in the country of spirit beings. The physical body comes about through the condensation of the human archetype to the point of sense-perceptibility, so we can also call this physical body a being of the first elemental kingdom condensed to the level of physical perceptibility. The ether body comes about when a form of the same origin remains mobile because of a being that extends its activity into the realm of sense-perceptibility but does not become perceptible itself. To characterize this being fully, we must say that it has its ultimate origin in the highest regions of the country of spirit beings and then takes shape in the second region as an archetype of life, which then works in the sense-perceptible world. In a similar way the being that builds up the sensing soul body also originates in the highest spirit regions, but takes shape in the third region as an archetype of the soul world and as such becomes active in the sense-perceptible world. The mind soul, however, comes about when the archetype of a thinking human being assumes the form of thought in the spirit world's fourth region and as such works directly in the sense-perceptible world.

This then, is how we human beings stand within the physical world, how the spirit works on our physical, ether and soul bodies and makes its appearance in our mind soul. Our three lower members are thus worked upon by archetypes in the form of beings that are external to us in a certain sense, but in our mind soul we begin to work consciously on ourselves. The beings that work on our physical body are the same ones that shape the minerals in nature. The ones that work on our ether body are the same kind as those that live in the plant kingdom, and the ones that work on our sentient soul body are the same kind as those that are active in the animal kingdom; both are invisible to sensory perception but extend their influence into these kingdoms.

[56]   We have now seen how the different worlds work together and how their working together expresses itself in the world in which we human beings live.

·   ·   ·

Having understood the sense-perceptible world in this [57] way, we are also open to understanding beings different from the ones that exist within the four kingdoms of nature. One example of this type of being is what we call our folk spirit, the spirit of our ethnic group or nation. This being does not appear directly in any sense-perceptible way. It lives and expresses itself in the sensations, feelings, inclinations, and so on, that we perceive as being shared by an entire ethnic group. It is a being that does not incarnate perceptibly as human beings do, but fashions its body out of the substances of the soul world. The soul body of the ethnic spirit surrounds the members of an ethnic group like a cloud in which they live; its influence becomes apparent in the souls of the individuals in question, but it does not originate in these souls. If we do not conceive of the ethnic spirit in this way, it will remain an empty abstraction, a schematic mental image devoid of life and being. Another example of this type of being is what we call the *Zeitgeist*, or spirit of an age. Indeed, our spiritual view widens to encompass a multitude of different higher and lower beings that live in our surroundings without becoming perceptible to our senses. However, those who are capable of spiritual perception do perceive these beings and can describe them.

The lower beings of this sort include all those described by seers as salamanders, sylphs, undines and gnomes. It should be unnecessary to mention at this point that such descriptions cannot be taken as literal depictions of the underlying reality. If they were, the world they refer to would not be a spiritual world but a crudely physical one. In fact, they illustrate a spiritual reality that can only be described by using metaphors and images. Individuals who accept sensory perception alone as valid will believe these beings to be the product of superstition and of an imagination run wild. This is totally under-standable. These beings will never become visible to physical eyes because they have no physical bodies. The superstition, however, lies not in believing these beings are real but in believing that they appear sense-percepti-bly. Beings of this sort help to build up the world, and we encounter them as soon as we enter higher territories that are inaccessible to our physical senses. The truly super-stitious people are not those who take these descriptions as images of spiritual realities, but both those who be-lieve in their actual physical existence and those who deny the spirit because they feel obliged to reject the sen-sory images.

Beings also exist who never descend into the soul world at all, but whose garments are woven out of the configurations of the country of spirit beings. We per-ceive them and become their companions when our spir-itual eyes and ears have been opened to them. This process enables us to understand many things we could formerly only stare at in total incomprehension. Light dawns around us; we see the causes of the effects and consequences that are played out in the physical world. We grasp things that formerly, when we lacked spiri-tual eyes, we either had to deny totally or dismiss with the saying, "There is more in heaven and earth than is dreamed of in your philosophy." People with a finer (that is, spiritual) sensitivity grow restless when they begin to be dimly aware of the presence of a world in addition to the sense-perceptible world around them, a world they have to feel their way around in, like blind people among visible objects. Clearly recognizing these higher regions of existence and penetrating what goes on in them with understanding is the only path that can really ground us and lead us toward our true calling as human beings. Through insight into what is concealed from our senses, we expand our own being in such a way that our life prior to this expansion seems to have been spent dreaming about the world.

VI. Thought Forms and the Human Aura

It has been said that the formations of any one of the three worlds are real for us only if we have the faculties or organs needed to perceive them. For example, certain processes taking place in space are perceptible to us as manifestations of light only because we have properly formed eyes. How much of what is real actually becomes evident to any being depends on that being's degree of receptivity. We are never justified in saying that only what we ourselves can perceive is real. Many things can be real, but we simply lack the organs to perceive them. [58]

The soul and spirit worlds are just as real as the sense-perceptible world; in fact, they are real in a much higher sense. No physical eye can see feelings and concepts, but they are real nonetheless. We encounter the phenomena of the physical world through our outer senses; similarly, feelings, impulses, instincts, thoughts and so on become perceptions for our spiritual organs. How these soul and spiritual phenomena become perceptions by means of our inner senses is analogous to how certain processes in space are perceived as colors. Of course, the full meaning of this statement can be understood only by those who have developed their inner senses by following the path to knowledge described in the next chapter. To such people, the soul phenomena of the soul environment and the spiritual phenomena of the spiritual region become supersensibly visible. They experience another being's feelings as raying out toward them like rays of light; when they turn their attention to others' thoughts, these thoughts radiate through spiritual space. For them, one person's thought about another person is not invisible, it is a perceptible process. The actual content of a thought exists only in the mind of the thinker, but it produces effects on the spiritual world and it is this process that is perceptible to the spiritual eye. The thought is an actual reality streaming out from one person toward the other, and how it affects the other person is experienced as a perceptible process in the spiritual world. For someone with opened spiritual senses, then, the physically perceptible person is only one part of the whole human being. The physical person is the center of soul and spiritual streams.

It is impossible to do more here than merely hint at the richly varied world that discloses itself to the seer. For example, a thought that is otherwise alive only in the listener's understanding appears as a spiritually perceptible color phenomenon, its color corresponding to the character of the thought. A thought stemming from a person's sensual impulses has a different tinge than one formulated in the service of pure knowledge, noble beauty or eternal truth. Thoughts springing from sensual activity move through the soul world in shades of red, while a thought that elevates the thinker to a higher form of knowledge appears in a beautiful shade of light yellow. One that stems from loving devotion discloses itself in a radiant rose-pink.[11] The supersensible manifestation of a thought expresses its degree of exactitude as well as its content. A thinking mind's precise thought appears as a formation with distinct contours, while a confused idea appears as a blurred and foggy formation.

In this way, a person's soul and spirit nature appear as the supersensible portion of a total human being. *[59]*

These spiritually perceptible colors, which surround an active physical human being like an egg-shaped cloud, constitute that person's aura. The size of this aura varies from person to person, but on the average we may imagine a whole person to be about twice as tall and four times as broad as his or her physical body. *[60]*

Within the aura, streams of different colors present a true and ever-changing picture of our inner life in all its variability. However, there are also some lasting basic *[61]*

---

11. Because these descriptions are obviously open to the crassest misinterpretation, a brief further commentary on them has been added at the end of this chapter.

colors that express specific permanent traits—talents, habits and idiosyncracies of character.

[62]   People who are currently far from being able to experience the path to knowledge described in the next chapter are likely to misunderstand the nature of what is described here as the "aura." They may imagine that the colors described here are present to our mind's eye in the same way that physical colors are present to our physical eyes. Such "soul colors," however, would be mere hallucinations. Spiritual science has absolutely nothing to do with hallucinatory impressions, and in any case that is not what is meant by these descriptions. We can get the right idea of what is meant if we keep in mind that we not only experience a sensory impression of a physical color, but also have a soul experience that is different when our souls—by means of our eyes—perceive a yellow surface than it is when we perceive a blue one. Let us call this experience "dwelling in yellow" or "dwelling in blue." A soul that has set out on the path to knowledge has this same experience of "dwelling in yellow" when it encounters the active soul experiences of other beings, and of "dwelling in blue" when it meets devotional attitudes. The point is not that seers visualizing another soul see "blue" in the same way they see it in the physical world, but rather that they have an experience that justifies their calling the visualization "blue," just as people who are perceiving physically call a blue curtain "blue," for example. Furthermore, seers must be aware that this is being experienced in a body-free state, so that they acquire the possibility of speaking about the value and significance of the soul's

life in a world *not* perceived through the medium of the human body. The sense in which this description is intended must be kept in mind, even though seers talk as a matter of course about "blue," "yellow" or "green" in an aura.

Human auras differ greatly according to individual differences in temperament, personality and degree of spiritual development. A person totally given over to animal impulses has a very different aura than someone who spends a lot of time thinking; a religious person's aura is fundamentally different from that of someone who is totally caught up in trivial daily events. In addition, all of a person's changing moods, inclinations, pleasures and pains are expressed in his or her aura. [63]

To learn what different shades of color in the aura signify, we must compare the auras of different types of mental and emotional experiences. We will first look at inner experiences that are penetrated through and through by pronounced emotions. These experiences can be separated into two different types. In one type, the soul is driven to these emotions primarily through the person's animal nature; in the other type, emotions assume a more refined form because they are strongly influenced by thinking and deliberation, so to speak. In the first type of experience, the streams of color flowing through particular parts of the aura are primarily various shades of brown and reddish yellow. In people with more refined emotions, shades of lighter reddish yellow, and also green, appear in the same places. It can be noted that shades of green appear more frequently with increasing intelligence. People who are [64]

highly intelligent but devote themselves totally to satisfying their animal impulses have a lot of green in their aura,
but this green always has a more or less pronounced tinge
of brown or brownish red. A large part of the aura of un-
intelligent people is flooded with streams that are brownish red or even dark blood-red.

[65]   The auras of emotional states such as these are fundamentally different from those of calm, contemplative,
thoughtful moods. There fewer brownish and reddish
tones are present, and various shades of green become
more pronounced. During strenuous thinking, the aura's
basic color becomes a pleasing green. This is especially
prominent in personalities who are said to be able to ad-
just to practically any situation in life.

[66]   Shades of blue appear during moods of devotion. The
more people place themselves in the service of a cause,
the more pronounced these shades of blue become. In this
connection, too, we may encounter two very different
types of people. The first type consists of passive people
who are not used to exerting their powers of thought, who
have only their good nature to throw into the flow of
world events, so to speak. Their auras glimmer with a
beautiful blue. This is also how many devotedly religious
personalities appear, as do compassionate natures and
people who devote themselves to leading a life of benev-
olence. If such people are also intelligent, blue streams al-
ternate with green, or the blue itself takes on a greenish
cast. In contrast to more passive personalities, more active people typically have their blue suffused from within
with light, bright tones. This is most clearly the case in

personalities we would call "wise" and especially in those who are full of fruitful ideas. In addition, everything that points to intellectual or spiritual activity generally takes the form of rays spreading out from within, while everything originating in animal vitality assumes the form of irregular clouds rolling through the aura.

According to whether the ideas that result from our emotional or mental activity serve our personal animalistic impulses or ideal and objective interests, the coloring of the corresponding auric formations will differ. An inventive mind that applies all its thoughts to satisfying its own sensuous passions shows dark shades of blue and red, while one that selflessly places its ideas at the service of an objective interest shows light red-blue tones. A life in the spirit that combines with noble devotion and capacity for self-sacrifice shows rosy pink or light violet colors. [67]

However, not only our underlying attitudes, but also our transient emotions, moods and other inner experiences are present as floods of color in our auras. A sudden outbreak of violent anger produces floods of red; a sudden upwelling of offended dignity appears as dark green clouds. And these color phenomena appear not only in irregular cloudlike formations, but also in figures of regular form and distinct limits. In the aura of a person suddenly seized with fear, we notice wavy stripes of blue with a reddish-blue shimmer moving from top to bottom. The aura of someone who is tensely awaiting some particular event has red-blue stripes constantly radiating from inside outward. [68]

[69]   Someone capable of precise spiritual perception can distinguish each impression another person receives from outside. People who get excited about every external impression have a constant flickering of little blue and red spots and flecks in their auras, while people who perceive less vividly have similar flecks that are yellow-orange or a lovely yellow color. The auras of so-called "absent-minded" people have bluish or blue-green specks of more or less variable shape.

[70]   Within the auric streams and rays surrounding a person, three different types of color phenomena are distinguishable to the more highly developed "spiritual eye." The first type of color is relatively dull and opaque in character, although even it seems fleeting and transparent in comparison to the type of color seen by our physical eyes. Within the spiritual world itself, however, these colors make the space they occupy comparatively opaque, as if they were filling it with figures of mist. The second type of color is all light, so to speak; these colors light up the space they occupy so that it too becomes all light. But the third type of color phenomenon is totally different from the other two in its radiating, sparkling, glittering character. These colors do not simply fill the space they light up; they shine and radiate right through it. There is something active and inwardly mobile about them, as if they were constantly creating themselves from within, while the other colors have something quieter and more lackluster about them. Figuratively speaking, the first two types of color fill space with a delicate fluid that quietly stays put, while the

third type fills it with constantly self-enkindling life and unceasing activity.

These three color types are not arranged in distinct layers in the human aura, nor do they occupy separate areas of space. Instead, they interpenetrate in a great variety of ways. It is possible to watch all three kinds mixing and mingling in the same place in the aura, just as a physical object such as a bell can be both seen and heard at the same time. This means that the aura is actually an incredibly complex phenomenon, because we are actually dealing with three interpenetrating auras. However, we can sort things out by turning our supersensible attention to only one of the three at a time. This is similar to shutting our eyes while listening intently to a piece of music in the sense-perceptible world. Seers have three different organs for the three kinds of color, so to speak, and can open one of them to impressions while closing the other two for the sake of undisturbed observation. To begin with, some seers may be able to see only one aura while the others remain invisible; others are receptive to the first two types but not to the third. The ability to observe all three auras, and to direct one's attention to one at a time for purposes of study, constitutes the higher stage of seership. *[71]*

The threefold human aura is the supersensibly perceptible expression of the three components of the human being's essential nature—body, soul and spirit. *[73]* The first aura reflects the body's influence on the soul; the second represents the soul's own life that extends beyond direct sensory stimulation but is not yet devoted to the service of the eternal; the third reflects the immortal *[72]* spirit's degree of mastery over the transitory aspect of human nature. It must be emphasized at this point that since these things are even more difficult to describe than they are to observe, this and any other attempt to describe auras should never be taken as anything more than a stimulus to understanding.

[74]   Thus, to a seer, the idiosyncracies of an individual's inner life are expressed in that person's auric makeup. Any emotional or mental activity that is totally given over to sensuous impulses, fleeting desires and momentary external stimuli shows up as garish colors in the first aura, while the second is weakly developed, showing mere traces of colored forms. In a case like this the third aura is barely visible. Only a flicker of color here and there indicates that even in a person with this attitude, the eternal is present in the form of potentials even though it may be suppressed by the effect of sensory factors. The more a person rids him- or herself of physical urges, the less prominent the first part of the aura becomes. Meanwhile, the second part becomes larger and larger, filling the body of colors within which the physical human being dwells with its radiating energy. And the more a person proves to be a servant of the eternal, the more the third part of the aura is revealed, showing the extent to which that individual is a citizen of the spiritual world. Through this part of the aura, an individual's divine self radiates into the earthly world. To the extent that individuals give evidence of this aura, they are flames used by the divinity to enlighten this world; through this part of the aura, they show the extent to which they work out of the eternally

true, beautiful and good, rather than out of themselves, the extent to which they have wrested from their narrower selves the capacity to offer themselves up on the great altar of cosmic activity. *[75]* Thus what individuals have made of themselves in the course of their incarnations comes to expression in their auras.

All three parts of the aura contain many different *[76]* shades of colors whose quality changes with an individual's degree of development. In the first portion, a person's undeveloped life of urges and impulses is seen in shades that range from red to blue. These shades are dull and opaque in quality. Pronounced shades of red point to sensual desires, lust and the pleasures of the palate. Shades of green appear primarily in characters with a tendency to apathy and indifference, lower natures who give themselves up greedily to any pleasures that come along but avoid the personal effort it would take to satisfy them. When a person's passions are intent on some goal beyond the reach of his or her acquired abilities, brownish green and yellowish green tints appear in the aura. This type of aura is fostered by certain modern lifestyles. *[77]* The lowest level of egotism—personal vanity rooted in low inclinations—is revealed in muddy yellow to brown tones.

But of course a life of animalistic urges also has a positive side. Even within the animal kingdom, a pure and natural capacity for self-sacrifice, of which instinctive mother-love is the most beautiful and highest expression, is evident to a great extent. Such selfless natural urges are expressed in the first aura in shades of light red to rose, while cowardly trepidation and a timid response to sensory stimuli show up as blue with a brownish or grayish cast.

[78]   Various grades of color are also apparent in the second aura. Brown and orange forms express strongly developed vanity, pride and ambition; red and yellow flecks point to curiosity. Green expresses an understanding of life and the world, while pale green reflects clear thinking and intelligence. Children who learn easily have a lot of green in this part of their auras. A greenish yellow coloring in the second aura points to a good memory. Rose pink indicates loving and benevolent wisdom, while blue is a sign of piety, verging on violet as this piety approaches religious fervor. Idealism and a serious, elevated outlook on life are seen as indigo blue.

[79]   In the third aura, the primary colors are yellow, green and blue. Here, light yellow appears when thinking is filled with elevated and comprehensive ideas that grasp the place of details in the divine order of the universe. In the case of intuitive thinking that has been purified of all sensory images, the yellow acquires a golden glow. Green expresses love for all beings; blue is the sign of willingness to make sacrifices for the sake of all. If this capacity for sacrifice intensifies into a forceful will that places itself actively in the service of the world, the blue becomes a light violet. If pride and ambition are still present as remnants of personal egotism in an otherwise highly developed soul, shades verging on orange appear in addition to the yellow. It is important to note, however, that the colors in this part of the aura are very different

from the shades we are used to seeing in the sense-perceptible world. The beauty and sublimity that meet us
here cannot be compared to anything in the ordinary
world.

This description of the aura cannot be properly assessed by anyone who does not place primary importance
on the fact that "seeing auras" signifies an expansion and
enrichment of our perception in the physical world. The
intent of this expanded perception is to recognize that
form of soul life which possesses spiritual reality outside
of the sense-perceptible world. What has been presented
here has nothing to do with reading a person's thoughts
or character from a hallucinatory aura and wants no deal-
ings with this questionable art. Its intent is to expand our
understanding in the direction of the spiritual world.

ADDENDUM

Of all the chapters in this book, this one on "Thought Forms and
the Human Aura" is probably the one most open to misinterpretation by opinions to the contrary, the one to which the most objections can be raised. For instance, it would be quite understandable
to insist that a seer's statements in this field be proved by experiments in line with scientific thinking, such as having a number of
people who claim to be able to see spiritual auras stand face to face
with a number of subjects whose auras they allow to work on
them. These seers should then report what thoughts, feelings, and
so on they saw in the auras of the people they observed. If their reports agree, and if it turns out that their subjects really did have the
feelings and thoughts ascribed to them, belief in the existence of
auras would seem reasonable. This is certainly the scientific way

to look at the issue. But something else must be taken into consideration. Spiritual researchers' work on their own souls gives them the capacity for spiritual vision; that is the point of their efforts. But whether they are then able to perceive something in the spiritual world in any given instance, and exactly what they perceive, does not depend on them but comes to meet them as a gift from the spiritual world. They cannot force it, they have to wait until it comes. Their intent to perceive spiritually is never the real cause of it happening, although that is what science would assume in the case of this experiment. The spiritual world will not allow itself to be bossed around. If this experiment were to come about at all, it would have to be initiated by the spiritual world, by a spiritual being's intention to reveal the thoughts of one or more subjects to one or more seers. A spiritual impulse would have to bring these seers together to carry out the observation, in which case their reports would be sure to agree. As paradoxical as it may seem to a strictly scientific mind, this is the fact of the matter. Spiritual experiments cannot come about in the same way as physical ones. If clairvoyants are visited by people they do not know, it cannot simply be assumed that they will be able to see the strangers' auras; it is not a matter of deliberate intent. They will be able to see them if and when there is a reason for it in the spiritual world.

The point of these few words is to draw attention to the misconception inherent in the objection described above. Spiritual science is meant to describe how people can learn to see and experience the reality of auras for themselves; all it can say to those who seek this knowledge is, "Apply these prerequisites to yourselves, and you too will see." It would certainly be more expedient if the demands of scientific thinking could be met, but those who require proofs of this sort have not familiarized themselves with even the most elementary results of spiritual science.

This book's statements about the human aura are not intended to accommodate spiritual sensation seekers who will be satisfied only by being presented with something "spiritual" that can be conceived of no differently than something physical—that is, when they can rest content in the sense world with their usual ideas. What was said at the beginning of this chapter about how auric color is to be imagined was surely calculated to prevent misunderstandings of this sort. But anyone who aspires to genuine spiritual insight has to realize that direct experience of matters of spirit and soul involves seeing the aura spiritually rather than sensorily. Without spiritual perception, the experience remains unconscious. We must not confuse the experience itself with its expression in pictorial form, but we must realize that the experience is very adequately expressed in this pictorial view. It is not something the perceiving soul makes up arbitrarily; it takes shape of itself in supersensible perception.

Scientists may be forgiven if they find themselves compelled to describe a human aura of some sort, as Dr. Moritz Benedikt does in his book on the rod and pendulum theory:

> There are a small number of people who are adapted to seeing in the dark. Of this minority, a relatively large percentage can see many objects in darkness but without colors, and only relatively few also see in colors.... My two classic cases of seeing in the dark examined a considerable number of scholars and physicians...in my darkroom, and these subjects were left with no justifiable doubt as to the accuracy of their observations and descriptions.... People who see colors in the dark see the front of the forehead and scalp as well as the rest of the righthand side in blue, while the left side is seen as red or sometimes...yellow and orange. The division and coloring are the same when seen from behind.*

*Moritz Benedikt, 1835-1920, physician. His book *Ruten und Pendellehre* (*The Rod and Pendulum Theory*) was published in Vienna in 1917; this quotation is from page 17.

Spiritual scientists, however, will not be forgiven so easily if they talk about auras.

But this author's intention is neither to take any kind of position on Benedikt's report—which is one of the most interesting in the annals of modern science—nor to grab at any flimsy opportunity to justify spiritual science by means of the natural sciences. His intent is only to point out how in one case someone investigating natural phenomena can make claims that are not totally dissimilar to those of spiritual science. It should be emphasized, however, that the aura discussed in this book is to be grasped by spiritual means and is something completely different from the one Benedikt is talking about, which can be studied by physical means. We would be surrendering to a gross illusion if we were to believe that spiritual auras could be investigated by any outer scientific methods. They are only accessible to the spiritual vision acquired on the path to knowledge described in the last chapter of this book. To recapitulate, the idea that the truth of spiritual perception can be verified in the same way that the truth of physical perception can, is based on a total misunderstanding.

CHAPTER 4

THE PATH
TO KNOWLEDGE

Each one of us is capable of coming to understand spiri- *[1]*
tual science as it is presented in this book. Explanations
such as those given here provide an image of the higher
worlds in thought form. In a certain respect, since we human beings are thinking beings, these very explanations
constitute a first step toward perceiving for ourselves. We
can only find our own path to knowledge by taking thinking itself as our starting point. To present our understanding with an image of higher worlds is by no means
fruitful, although at the immediate moment it may indeed be no more than an account of things we are not yet
able to perceive for ourselves. Thoughts that have been
supplied for us constitute a force that goes on working in
the world of our thoughts. This force becomes active
within us, arousing potentials that lie dormant in us. It is
a mistake to believe that we waste our time by dwelling
on an image in thought form. This opinion assumes that
thoughts are unreal and abstract, while in actuality they

are founded on a living force. To someone who has acquired knowledge, thoughts are present as a direct expression of what is perceived in the spirit, and when this expression is communicated to a second person, it lives on in that person as a seed that will grow and bear knowledge as its fruit. Anyone who scorns strenuous mental effort as a way of acquiring higher knowledge, turning instead to other forces available to us, is not taking into account the fact that thinking is the highest of the faculties we human beings possess in the physical world.

For this reason, people who ask how to acquire direct higher spiritual scientific knowledge should be told to begin by familiarizing themselves with what others have to say about it. If they insist that they want only to see for themselves, that they do not want to know about what other people have seen, they must be told that learning what others have to say on the subject is the first step toward acquiring knowledge for themselves. Of course they may say that meanwhile they are forced to accept things on blind faith. However, the point is not to believe or disbelieve what has been communicated, but only to be unbiased and receptive toward it. Genuine spiritual researchers never speak in the expectation that they will be met with blind faith, but say only, "These are my experiences in spiritual areas of existence, and I am simply telling you about them." However, they also know that opening oneself to this information and imbuing one's own thoughts with it constitute active forces for spiritual development in the listener.

[2]   To approach this issue correctly, we must take into account that all knowledge of the soul and spirit worlds

lies dormant in each human soul and can be brought to light by traveling the path to knowledge. However, we are capable of grasping not only what we ourselves bring up from the soul's depths, but also what someone else has done in this respect. This is true even if we ourselves have not set out on the path to knowledge. Correct spiritual insight awakens the power of understanding in any mind not clouded by prejudice, and our own subconscious knowledge readily acknowledges spiritual facts discovered by others. This is no blind faith, but rather the natural response of common sense. What our healthy natural understanding recognizes as true when presented with the results of genuine spiritual research constitutes a much better starting point for firsthand knowledge of the spiritual world than any dubious mystical contemplations and the like, even though we often assume the opposite.

The need to subject ourselves to the hard work of think- *[3]* ing if we want to develop our capacity for higher knowledge cannot be emphasized strongly enough. This is all the more urgent because many people who want to become seers underestimate the need for this earnest and self-denying work on one's thinking. They say that thinking doesn't work for them, that everything depends on "feeling," or the like. These people must be told that it is impossible to become a seer in the true higher sense of the word without first working one's way into the world of thinking. A certain inner laziness plays a regrettable role in many personalities, who do not become aware of it because it disguises itself as contempt for abstract thinking and for idle speculation, and so on. However, we completely misunderstand thinking if we confuse it with any idle or abstract spinning of thoughts. That kind of "abstract thinking" can easily kill supersensible knowledge, but living, vital thinking can become the foundation for it.

Of course it would be much more comfortable if we could avoid the strenuous work of thinking while acquiring the higher faculties of a seer, and many people would prefer to do it that way. However, only thinking can lead to the inner steadiness and stability of soul that seership requires. Without it, we get nothing more than a meaningless and erratic display of images—enjoyable, perhaps, but totally irrelevant as far as actual access to the higher world is concerned. And if we consider the purely spiritual experiences of an individual who really enters the higher world, we will also grasp still another side of the issue. An absolutely healthy soul life is essential for a seer, and there is no better means of cultivating a healthy soul life than real thinking. In fact, people's mental health can suffer seriously if their training for higher development is not based on thinking. Becoming a seer will make any healthy right-thinking individual even healthier and more fit for life than before, but taking a dreamy approach to self-development by shunning the rigors of thinking can only foster illusions and a faulty approach to life. There is no need to worry, however, as long as what has been said here is taken into account as a prerequisite to higher development, a prerequisite that has to do exclusively with the human soul and spirit. Once this prerequisite is recognized, to talk about any possible harmful effect on a person's bodily health is absurd.

Unwarranted disbelief, however, *is* harmful because it [4] acts as a repelling force, preventing the recipient from taking up the fruitful influence of these thoughts. The prerequisite to opening our higher senses is not blind faith, but simply receptivity to the world of spiritual scientific thought. Spiritual researchers challenge their students, not to *believe* what they are told, but to *think* it, to take it into the world of their own thoughts. By allowing it to work from within, they will come to recognize its truth on their own. This is the approach spiritual researchers take—they provide the incentive, but the power to perceive the truth arises within the listeners themselves. This is how spiritual scientific ideas ought to be sought. Those who have the self-discipline to immerse their thoughts in spiritual science can be sure that this will eventually lead to the ability to perceive for themselves.

What has just been said already suggests one of the first [5] qualities that must be cultivated by people who want to achieve independent perception of higher realities. It is *unreserved and unbiased devotion* to what human life or the world outside us has to reveal. If we approach any phenomenon with a preconceived notion derived from our life as it has been until now, we shut ourselves off from the quiet yet pervasive influence this phenomenon can have on us. While learning, we must be able at any moment to make ourselves into a totally empty vessel into which the world we do not know can flow. Moments of recognition happen only when any prejudice or criticism coming from us is silenced. For instance, it makes no difference whether we are wiser than the person we are meeting—even a child with minimal understanding has something to disclose to the greatest sage. Approaching the child with any prejudgment at all, no matter how wise, is like looking "through a glass, darkly" at what the child has to reveal.[1]

Complete inner selflessness is part of this devotion to what the unknown world can reveal, and we will probably make some astonishing discoveries about ourselves when we test the extent of our own devotion. If we want to set out on the path to higher knowledge, we must practice until we are able to obliterate ourselves and all our prejudices at any moment so that something else can flow into us. Only high levels of selfless devotion enable us to perceive the higher spiritual phenomena all around us. We can deliberately cultivate this faculty by trying to refrain from judging people in our surroundings, for example. We must eliminate any standards of attractiveness and unattractiveness, stupidity and cleverness, that we apply as a matter of habit. We must try to understand people purely out of themselves. It is best to practice on people to whom we have an active aversion, forcibly suppressing this aversion and letting everything they do work on us without bias. Or if we find ourselves in some circumstances that elicit a certain judgment in response, we can suppress this judgment in order to be receptive

---

1. It is evident from this example that there can be no question of erasing our own judgment or submitting to blind faith—this would make no sense in reference to a child.

and unbiased toward any impressions that may come to us.[2]

We should allow things and events to speak to us more than we speak about them, and we should extend this principle to our thoughts as well, suppressing whatever it is in ourselves that shapes a certain thought and allowing only external things to elicit thoughts. Exercises like this can help us achieve our goal of higher knowledge only if they are carried out with persistence and in holy earnestness. Anyone who underestimates exercises of this sort is totally unaware of their value. On the other hand, anyone experienced in these matters knows that devotion and absence of bias actually create strength. Just as the heat that is applied to a boiler is transformed into the force that makes a steam engine move, these exercises in selfless spiritual devotion are transformed within us into the strength to see into the spiritual worlds.

By means of this exercise, we make ourselves receptive *[6]* to everything around us, but receptivity is not enough. We must also be capable of properly assessing what we perceive. As long as we still tend to overvalue ourselves at the expense of the world around us, we are putting off the moment when we will gain access to higher knowledge. People who give in to the personal pleasure or pain they experience through things and events in the outer

---

2. This unbiased receptivity has nothing to do with blind faith. The point is not to believe blindly in something, but rather to refrain from letting "blind judgment" usurp the place of a living and vital impression.

world are still caught up in valuing themselves too highly. Their personal pleasure or pain teaches them something about themselves but nothing about the things in question. If I am sympathetically inclined toward someone, my own relationship to that person is all I can experience at first. And if I allow my judgment and my behavior to depend on my own feelings of pleasure or sympathy, I allow my own idiosyncracies to take center stage and impose them on my surroundings. I want the world to include me just as I am, but I do not want to accept the world for what it is or to let it assert itself in accordance with the forces at work in it. In other words, I am tolerant of only what suits my own personality; I ward off anything else. And as long as we remain captives of the sense world, we are especially likely to ward off any non-sensory influences.

As we learn, we must develop the ability to relate to things and people in their uniqueness, recognizing the value and significance of each and every one. Sympathy and antipathy, pleasure and displeasure, must take on totally new roles. This is clearly not a matter of completely eradicating sympathy and antipathy and becoming totally numb to them. On the contrary, the more we cultivate our ability to refrain from responding immediately to sympathy or antipathy with a judgment or an action, the finer the sensitivity we develop. Once we can control the character they already assume within us, we will experience that sympathies and antipathies assume a higher character. Even the seemingly most unappealing thing has hidden qualities that are revealed when we do not simply yield to our own selfish feelings. People who have schooled themselves in this regard are exceptionally sensitive to everything around them because they do not allow their own inclinations to make them unreceptive. Any inclination we follow blindly deadens our ability to see things around us in the right light; it makes us force our way through our environment rather than exposing ourselves to it and experiencing its inherent value.

Once we no longer react selfishly to each instance of joy and pain, sympathy and antipathy, we become independent of the changing impressions we receive from the outer world. The pleasure we experience because of a particular thing immediately makes us dependent on that thing; we lose ourselves in it. We cannot travel the path to higher knowledge if we are constantly losing ourselves in either pleasure or pain as a result of the ever-changing impressions that confront us. Once we have learned to accept pleasure and pain with equanimity, we can stop losing ourselves in them and begin to understand them. As soon as I surrender to pleasure, it consumes my very existence. Instead, I should make use of pleasure only as a means of understanding pleasurable things. The point for me should not be the fact that something causes me pleasure; I should experience the pleasure and, through it, the nature of the thing itself. For me, pleasure should be nothing more than an indication that this thing possesses the ability to give pleasure, a characteristic I must learn to recognize in it. If I stop short at the pleasure itself and let myself be totally taken in by it, I am experiencing only myself; on the other hand, if pleasure gives me an opportunity to experience a [7] characteristic of the thing itself, I enrich my inner nature through the experience. In the course of our research, pleasure and displeasure, joy and pain, must present us with opportunities to learn about things. This does not make us immune to pleasure and pain; it enables us to rise above them so that they can disclose the actual nature of external things. By cultivating this faculty, we will come to realize what good teachers pleasure and pain are. We will co-experience what each and every being feels and thus receive a revelation of its inner nature.

If we are truly seeking, we never stop short at our own suffering or pleasure, but always ask what that joy or suffering has to tell us. We surrender our personal selves so that suffering or pleasure coming from the outside world can work on us. This permits us to develop a totally new way of relating to things. Whereas our reactions to specific impressions used to be based only on our own liking or disliking, we can now let pleasure and displeasure be organs through which things tell us what they themselves are in their essence. In us, pleasure and pain are transformed from mere feelings into sensory organs through which we perceive the outer world. When our eyes see something, they do not take action themselves but rather cause our hands to act. So, too, when a spiritual researcher's pleasure and pain (to the extent that they are being applied as a means to knowledge) receive impressions, they do not act directly; only what is experienced via pleasure and displeasure then leads to action. When we make a practice of using pleasure and displeasure as organs to transmit information, they fashion the actual soul organs we need for the soul world to disclose itself to us. Our eyes can serve our physical body only by being organs of transmission for sensory impressions; similarly, pleasure and displeasure develop into "soul eyes" when they cease to assert themselves for their own sake and begin to reveal unknown souls to us.

The above-mentioned faculties put us in a position to [8] let the things and beings present in our surroundings work on us free of the disturbing influence from our own idiosyncrasies. But we must also insert ourselves into the spiritual world, of which we all, as thinking beings, are citizens. This can happen in the right way only if, during the process of recognizing the spirit, we can make our train of thought correspond to the eternal laws of truth, the laws of spirit country. This is the only way this world can work on us and reveal its phenomena to us.

We will not reach the truth by simply giving ourselves up to the transient thoughts coursing through our "I." These thoughts have their progression imposed on them in that they come into existence within our bodily nature. As long as the physical brain is conditioning our cognitive activity, our thoughts appear haphazard and confused—one thought begins and then breaks off, driven from the scene by a second thought. If we really examine a conversation between two people as we listen to it, or if we observe ourselves carefully, we will get an idea of the will-o'-the-wisp quality of these thoughts. As long as we are applying ourselves to tasks in the sense-perceptible world, our confused train of thought is always straightened out by the actual matter at hand. Regardless of how confused I am in my thinking, daily life forces me to conform to the laws of reality in my actions. For example, I may have an extremely haphazard idea of how a city is laid out, but if I want to get around in it, I have to adapt to how things really are. Mechanics may come into the shop with their heads full of a jumble of all kinds of ideas, but the laws governing how their machines work will compel them to adopt appropriate working procedures. In the sense-perceptible world, hard facts act as a constant corrective to our thinking. If I have the wrong idea about some physical phenomenon such as the form of a plant, reality confronts me and sets my thinking straight.

In relationship to higher areas of existence, however, things are very different. These realms disclose themselves to me only when I approach them with my thinking already strictly disciplined. In this case, if my thinking does not provide the correct impulse, if I am not my own confident guide, I will not find the right way to go. The spiritual laws prevailing here have not condensed to the point of physical perceptibility and therefore do not impose the same corrective as sense-perceptible things do, so I will be able to obey them only if they are related to my own laws, the ones that govern me as a thinking being. As a seeker of knowledge, I must alter my thinking so that it is strictly self-regulating. My thoughts must gradually get out of the habit of running their everyday course and adopt instead the inner character of the spiritual world. I must be able to observe myself in this regard and keep things under control. I must not allow one thought to follow another arbitrarily but only in accordance with the rigorous standards of the contents of the thought world. The transition from one idea to another must correspond to strict laws of thinking, and I myself as a thinker must stand as a copy of these laws, so to speak. I must eliminate from my train of thought everything not flowing from these laws. If a favorite thought gets in my way, I must push it aside so that it does not disturb the orderly sequence, and if a personal feeling tries to impose a direction on my thoughts that is not inherent in them, I must suppress it.

Plato required those applying to his school to take a course in mathematics first. Since the strict laws of mathematics are not subject to the ordinary course of sensory phenomena, they make a very good preparation for seekers of knowledge, who must put aside personal arbitrariness and distractions if they wish to make progress in mathematics. Voluntarily overcoming all uncontrolled and arbitrary thinking prepares them for the task ahead. They learn to respond to only the requirements of thinking itself, since that is how they must proceed in all thought activity that serves spiritual knowledge. Their thinking must replicate the undisturbed results and conclusions of mathematics. Wherever they go, wherever they may be, they must always attempt to think in this way. Then the laws of the spiritual world, laws that pass through without a trace when thinking is of the everyday confused variety, can flow into them. Well-ordered thinking leads them from secure starting points to the most hidden truths. (These suggestions should not be taken one-sidedly, however—although mathematics is good practice and discipline for our thinking, it is certainly possible to learn pure, healthy and vital thinking without it.)

[9]   Seekers of knowledge must have the same goals for their actions as they have for their thinking—that is, their actions must not be disrupted by their personality, but must be able to obey the laws of eternal beauty and truth, accepting the direction these laws provide. Knowledge seekers who have begun something they recognize as right may not give up simply because what they are doing is not emotionally satisfying. On the other hand, they may not continue with something just because they enjoy it if they discover that it does not conform to the laws of eternal beauty and truth. In everyday life, people let their actions be determined by what is personally satisfying or fruitful; they impose the direction of their own personality on the course of world events. They are doing nothing to bring about the truth laid out in the laws of the spiritual world; they are simply fulfilling their own arbitrary demands. We are acting in harmony with the spiritual world only when its laws are the only ones we obey. Actions proceeding only from our own personality supply no forces that could form a basis for spiritual knowledge.

Seekers of knowledge cannot consider only what will yield fruit or lead to success for themselves; they must also consider what they have recognized as good. They must willingly submit to the strict law that requires them to renounce all personal arbitrariness and all fruits their actions may have for their own personality. Then they are walking the paths of the spiritual world and their whole being is permeated by its laws. They are freed from all sensory constraints; their spirit being lifts free of its sensory trappings. This is how they spiritualize themselves, how they make progress toward the spiritual.

We cannot question whether it does any good to resolve to obey only the laws of truth when in fact we may be mistaken about what is true. Everything depends on our effort and our attitude, and even people who are mistaken but are aspiring to the truth possess a strength that will set them back on the right track. The very objection that we may be mistaken is in itself destructive disbelief and demonstrates a lack of trust in the power of truth. The point here is that instead of presuming to decide on our goals from our own self-serving point of view, we should submit selflessly to the spirit and allow it to determine our direction for us. Self-serving human volition cannot dictate to the truth. Truth itself must become sovereign in us, filling our whole being and transforming us into a replica of spirit country's eternal laws. We must imbue ourselves with these eternal laws in order to let them flow out into life. As seekers of knowledge, we must have our will as well as our thinking strictly under control. Then, in all humility and without presumption, we become messengers of the world of truth and beauty. We advance to become participants in the spiritual world and are lifted from one level of development to the next. But we cannot achieve living in the spirit merely by being beholders of it—it has to be experienced.

If the laws that are presented here are observed by *[10]* seekers of knowledge, their inner experience in relation to the spiritual world will assume a completely new form. Instead of having significance only for their own personal life, it will develop into soul perceptions of the higher world. Feelings of pleasure and displeasure or joy and pain will grow into soul organs that transmit outer impressions selflessly like physical eyes and ears, which also do not exist for themselves alone. This is how knowledge seekers achieve the calm and secure frame of mind required for research in the spiritual world. A great pleasure that once would have simply made them jump for joy will now alert them to previously unnoticed aspects of their surroundings and will leave them at peace. Within this peace, features of the entities causing the pleasure will be revealed. And on the other hand, pain will no longer simply fill the seekers with distress but will also be able to inform them what qualities belong to the being causing the pain. Like eyes, which desire nothing for themselves but selflessly show the physical person what direction to take, pleasure and pain will lead the soul safely on its way.

This is the state of inner equanimity that we as seekers of knowledge must achieve. When pleasure and pain no longer expend themselves in creating turbulence in our inner life, they begin to function like eyes open to the supersensible world. It is not possible to use pleasure and pain as sources of information as long as we are dwelling in and on them, but once we have learned to live *through* them and no longer relate our feeling of identity to them, they become organs of perception we can use in order to see and to know. It is incorrect to think that a sage must become a dry, sober person incapable of experiencing pleasure or pain. For such a person, pleasure and pain still exist, but when he or she is investigating the spiritual world, these are present in metamorphosed form as "eyes and ears."

As long as our relationship to the world is a personal one, things show us only what connects them to our own personality. This, however, is merely their transient aspect. If we pull back from what is transient in ourselves and dwell with our "I" and our feeling of identity in what is lasting in us, our transient features are transformed and begin to convey the eternal aspects of things to us. This relationship between our own eternal aspect and what is eternal in other things is something seekers must be able to bring about deliberately. Before taking up any other exercises of the sort described here, and also while practicing them, we need to direct our attention to this immortal aspect. Whenever I observe a stone, plant, animal or person, I should be aware that something eternal is expressed there. I should be able to wonder about what is lasting in a transitory stone or a mortal person, what it is that will outlast their transient sense-perceptible manifestation.

[11]

We must not imagine that if we turn our mind to the eternal like this, it will estrange us from immediate reality and destroy our ordinary capacity for observation and our feeling for everyday affairs. On the contrary! Each little leaf and beetle will reveal countless mysteries when we look at it not only with our eyes but also, through our eyes, with our spirit as well. Every glimmer or shade of color, every intonation, will remain vividly perceptible to our senses. Nothing will be lost, but infinite new life will be gained. People who do not know how to observe the smallest detail with their eyes will also never achieve spiritual vision, but only pale and bloodless thoughts. Everything depends on the attitude we acquire.

How far we get will depend on our abilities. We only have to do what is right and let the rest develop on its own. To begin with, we must be content with turning our attention to what is lasting; this effort in and of itself will eventually allow us to recognize the eternal. We must wait until this is given to us. It will happen at the right moment if we wait—and *work*. Soon after beginning such exercises, people notice major inner transformations. They learn to base their estimation of a thing's importance or lack of it exclusively on its recognized relationship to something lasting and eternal. They arrive at a new and different assessment of the world and feel differently related to their surroundings. What is transitory no longer attracts them for its own sake, as it used to, but becomes both part of and a metaphor for the eternal. They learn to love the eternal that lives in everything; it becomes as familiar to them as only the transitory aspect was before. This does not estrange them from life; on the contrary, they learn to value each thing in accordance with its true significance. Even life's trivial aspects do not leave such people untouched, but instead of getting lost in frivolities, spirit-seeking individuals see them in the right light and recognize their limited value. It would be a poor seeker of knowledge who would prefer to roam the cloudy heights and lose touch with life.

True seers know how to use their elevated vantage point, clear overview and strong sense of what is important to put each thing in its right place.

The spiritually knowledgeable become able to stop obeying only the outer sense world's unpredictable influences that direct their intentions this way and that. Knowledge lets them see into the eternal nature of things; through transforming their inner world, they have acquired the ability to perceive this eternal nature. The following thoughts acquire a particular significance for those who truly know. While acting out of themselves, such people are aware of acting out of the eternal nature of things, for they know that it is within them that outer things express their essence. Therefore, when the knowers' activity is directed by the eternal that lives within them, they are acting in accordance with the eternal order of the universe. They know that they are no longer simply being impelled by things but are actively impelling things according to the laws implanted in the things themselves, laws which have also become the laws of their own being.

This acting from within can only be an ideal to strive for—reaching the goal still lies in the distant future, but the seeker of knowledge must have the will to see the way clearly. This is the *will to freedom*, because freedom means acting from within, and only those who draw their motivation from the eternal can work from within. Any being who does not do this works out of reasons other than those inherent in things themselves and thus works contrary to the order of the universe, which will triumph

[12]

in the end. Ultimately, that is, this being cannot get its way and cannot become free. Arbitrary individual volition annihilates itself through the effect of its actions.

• • •

[13]   Those who can work on their inner life in this way advance from stage to stage in spiritual knowledge. As a fruit of their exercises, specific insights into the supersensible world become accessible to their spiritual perception. They learn the sense in which facts about this world are to be taken and confirm them through direct experience. Having reached this stage, they are approached by something that can be encountered only along this path. In a way whose significance can only now become clear to them, "initiation" is bestowed on them through the great spiritual powers guiding the human race; they become disciples of wisdom. The less we see this initiation as consisting of any outward human relationship, the more accurate the idea we have of it.

It is possible only to hint at what is now happening to seekers of knowledge. They acquire a new home and become conscious inhabitants of the supersensible world. From now on, their spiritual insight flows from a higher source. The light of knowledge no longer shines toward them from outside; they themselves stand at this light's source. They see the riddles that the world presents in a new light. Now they converse not with things that have been given form by the spirit but with the formative spirit itself. In moments of spiritual knowledge, their life as personalities exists only to serve as a conscious metaphor of the eternal. They can no longer have any doubts about the spirit, because doubt is possible only for someone whom things mislead with regard to the spirit that prevails within them. And since the disciples of wisdom are able to converse with the spirit itself, any false form in which they previously imagined the spirit vanishes. Imagining the spirit in a false form is superstition, and initiates are beyond superstition because they know what the true form of the spirit is.

Freedom from the biases of personality, doubt and superstition characterize those who have traveled up the path of knowledge to the level of discipleship, but we must not confuse this uniting of personalities with the surrounding and all-encompassing spiritual life with the dissolution or destruction of personality in a universal spirit. That is not what happens in true personality development. Personality as such is maintained on entering into relationship with the spirit world; it is not overcome, but undergoes still higher development. If we need a metaphor of what happens when individual spirits unite with the universal spirit, we must not imagine different circles that coincide and become one, but many overlapping circles, each with a distinct shade of color. Although the circles overlap, each individual shade maintains its identity within the whole, and no circle loses any of the fullness of its individual strength.

No further description of this path will be given here. *[14]* To the extent that this is possible, it is done in *Occult Science*, which is a sequel to this volume.

What has been said here about the path to spiritual knowledge can all too easily be misinterpreted as advocating the cultivation of moods and attitudes that entail turning away from the immediate, joyful and active experience of life. It must be emphasized that the inner attitude that renders our soul fit for direct experience of spiritual reality cannot by extension be required of all the rest of our life. Those who investigate existence in the spirit can indeed achieve the soul distance from sensory reality necessary for their research without becoming strangers to the world on a general level. On the other hand, we must also realize that knowledge of the spiritual world that is acquired either through actually setting out on this path or through simply grasping spiritual scientific truths with our unprejudiced and healthy common sense does lead to higher moral standards, to an understanding of sensory existence as it accords with the truth, to a secure confidence in life and to mental health.

RELATED READING

The Philosophy of Freedom (1894)

In this early work, Steiner lays down the prerequisites for a path of brain- or sense-free thinking. Anyone wishing to understand the epistemological foundations that underlie Steiner's powers of spiritual-scientific observation should read this work.

How to Know Higher Worlds (1904)

Previously titled *Knowledge of the Higher Worlds and Its Attainment*, this is Rudolf Steiner's classic account of the modern path of initiation.

Occult Science (1910)

Originally conceived of as a continuation of *Theosophy*, this work deals with the nature and evolution of humanity and the cosmos. It also extends and deepens many of the areas dealt with in *Theosophy*. It contains a description of the path of knowledge, including the "Rose Cross meditation," which complements and adds to the descriptions contained in *Theosophy* and *How to Know Higher Worlds*.

A Road to Self Knowledge and *The Threshold of the Spiritual World.*

This work makes available much of the fundamental content of anthroposophy in the form of meditations.

The Spiritual Guidance of the Individual and Humanity

This small work begins to indicate the role of Christ in human nature and human evolution.

The Foundations of Esotericism (1905); *At the Gates of Spiritual Science (*1906); *Theosophy of the Rosicrucian* (1907)

These three lecture courses deal with many of the same areas as *Theosophy*. Readers will find much additional food for thought here, sometimes in more easily digestible form.

The Influence of Spiritual Beings on Man (1908)

Concerning various facts and beings of the higher worlds and their connection with humanity.

An Occult Physiology (1911)

Deals in greater detail with the connection of cosmic and spiritual processes to human physiology.

Spiritual Beings in the Heavenly Bodies and in the Kingdoms of Nature (1912)

This contains important observations on the connection between the various spiritual hierarchies and the bodies, as well as the I, of the human being.

The Effects of Spiritual Development on the Occult Sheaths of Man (1913)

Inner development transforms all aspects of the human being. This lecture course shows the different ways in which various spiritual practices effect the human constitution.

Chance, Providence, and Necessity (1915)

These lectures, above all, focus on the etheric nature of the human being that unites the human being and the cosmos, and especially on the etheric body as the instrument of perception for imaginative cognition.

The Human Being in Body, Soul, and Spirit (1922)

Simple and direct, these lectures were given to the workers constructing the Goetheanum in Dornach.

Anthroposophy and the Inner Life (1924)

Previously titled *Anthroposophy, an Introduction,* this work approaches the subject matter of *Theosophy* from "within." It gives, as it were, the inner meaning of *Theosophy* in terms of closely observed experiences of consciousness.

––––––––––––––––––––

The following titles deal with questions of reincarnation, karma, and life between death and rebirth, as discussed in *Theosophy*, Chapters Two and Three:

Rosicrucian Esotericism (1909)

Manifestations of Karma (1910)

Reincarnation and Karma (1912)

Life Between Death and Rebirth (1912-13)

Between Death and Rebirth (1912-13)

––––––––––––––––––––

All works by Rudolf Steiner that are in print are available from SteinerBooks [Anthroposophic Press] www.steinerbooks.org. For out of print works, write: Rudolf Steiner Library, 65 Fern Hill Road, Ghent, NY 12075.

DURING THE LAST TWO DECADES of the nineteenth century the Austrian-born Rudolf Steiner (1861–1925) became a respected and well-published scientific, literary, and philosophical scholar, particularly known for his work on Goethe's scientific writings. After the turn of the century he began to develop his earlier philosophical principles into an approach to methodical research of psychological and spiritual phenomena.

His multifaceted genius has led to innovative and holistic approaches in medicine, science, education (Waldorf schools), special education, philosophy, religion, economics, agriculture (Biodynamic method), architecture, drama, new arts of eurythmy and speech, and other fields. In 1924 he founded the General Anthroposophical Society, which today has branches throughout the world.